Forever Our Angels

By

Hannah Stone

In Appreciation

This book, if you will pardon the pun, has been a labor of mine since my first pregnancy loss in 1994. I owe a great deal of gratitude to the men and women who contributed their personal stories of pregnancy loss. As difficult as it was, each contributor relived the pain and heartache of a pregnancy loss (or losses) of the past, in order to help others in the present and future. Their willingness to speak out and be heard has been inspiration to me and I'm sure, to the readers of this book.

My doctor was a wonderful support system to my husband and me when we suffered our second and third pregnancy losses. Whether it was holding my hand and giving me a hug or calling us to offer his personal support, he went beyond the call of duty.

I befriended Alan and Dr. Sara Goldman during their own time of loss. Though we have sons in the same class, we did not truly get to know each other until I told them about this book I wanted to write. Alan encouraged me to resume this project after a six year hiatus while Sara graciously agreed to write the introduction to this book. Together as a couple, they have been dealt the blow of four pregnancy losses and have come out all the more strong.

My parents experienced the pain along with my husband and me with each and every loss. They listened when we needed to speak and they spoke words of comfort when we needed to hear. I am a better mother because I learned from the best of parents.

My husband has been my biggest supporter in everything that I do. He and I experienced each pregnancy loss as a team. Though I had suffered both physically and emotionally with each loss, I know that he felt no less in his sorrow. Sharing our losses together as a couple has only made us stronger and more committed to one another. To him, I say I love you. I couldn't ask for a more perfect husband and father to our children.

My children are the jewels in my life and a gift that I treasure each and every day. To each of them, I say, I love you more than you love me.

Someone wise once said that it takes a village to raise a child. I say, it takes a village to make a child. In my own village, I have many friends and extended family members who have provided my husband and me with love and support during our losses. Whether it was a simple hug or cooking a meal or offering words of sympathy, they were there.

ISBN 1-4116-7073-6 34468651 10/06

Introduction
by
Dr. Sara Goldman

It is estimated that anywhere from 12% to 50% of all pregnancies end in first or second trimester loss. In addition, women with three or more losses have a miscarriage rate of 30% to 40%. Yet talking about pregnancy loss remains shrouded in mystery both within the medical community and among women who have suffered losses. This makes going through a pregnancy loss a frightening, isolating experience for most women. Upon a woman's return home from the hospital, a pregnancy loss is usually not talked about, particularly if the loss was during the first trimester, when a woman may have not yet told others about her pregnancy. Often, the only solace women find is in furtive conversations between close friends. I have had this experience, both personally and professionally. For that reason, I was very pleased to have been asked to write an introduction to Hannah Stone's ground-breaking book. It is a wonderful beginning to lifting the silence surrounding pregnancy loss.

I was, at first, surprised and then dismayed when I began to search for articles among the medical community about pregnancy loss and grief. No matter how many different ways I tried to search, the main body of literature was in the nursing field with very little mention of the issues of grieving written by or for physicians. And this, indeed, parallels my own experience of loss. As a psychiatrist who suffered four pregnancy losses (two of them in the second trimester), I found that even the most caring obstetrician was uncomfortable in helping me navigate my grief. The most meaningful help I received in the hospital was from a sensitive and caring nursing staff, which made a tremendous difference in helping me with my pain. Yet, I wished my obstetrician had been involved in helping to educate me about what to expect from my grief. Even my training as a psychiatrist had not prepared me for such an experience.

When I returned home from the hospital, I found that most people, while quite supportive, were uncomfortable in openly addressing my losses. But women began to talk to me in private and I discovered that many more women than I had ever realized have experienced pregnancy losses. They, too, felt that there was nowhere to turn to feel less alone with their loss. Although nothing can remove the pain, the proper treatment and acknowledgement of such a loss can ultimately ease the burden of suffering and can help a woman experience her loss in a healthy way which prevents grieving from becoming pathological. All such help begins with openness and education.

Therefore, I want to present a brief outline of the forms grief can take and of the interventions that can be helpful, both during a pregnancy loss and in its aftermath. These interventions should begin with the physician but can be continued by the people within a woman's support system through their openness and support. It is our hope that this book be a place for men and women to turn to for such support, to help bring the feelings experienced after a pregnancy loss out in the open and to inform women going through a loss such that they are not alone.

In her classic book "On Death and Dying," Elisabeth Kubler-Ross delineates five stages that those faced with death experience: denial and isolation, anger, bargaining, depression and acceptance, which may exist alone or side by side, in any order. Although Ross' original work was done with terminally ill cancer patients, it is universally recognized that all who suffer loss go through these stages, be it loss of limb, of health, of a loved one or of a pregnancy.

In order to successfully navigate the stages of grieving and finally arrive at acceptance, the support of others in helping the bereaved work through their emotions is crucial. The authors of a 2003 Swedish study in which 15 women were interviewed post-loss reported that for those women who were not encouraged to grieve, pregnancy loss "festered." Although they were able to return to everyday life, they had not been able to talk with others and achieve resolution. This type of hidden loss, referred to as "unresolved grief," often leads to increased depression, distress, and chronic mourning. It can even lead to complicated bereavement, in which the normal grieving pattern is interrupted with resultant psychiatric symptoms such as severe depression and psychosis. In order to facilitate healthy grieving, support and validation by others is almost always required.

Studies have shown that women experience many emotions following a pregnancy loss but the most common emotions are grief, guilt, emptiness, loss and abandonment. Men tend to experience less intense grief reactions, the strength of which seems to correlate with the gestational age of the baby at the time of the loss. Attention must be paid to their grief as well, since they are subject to the same complications as women, whose grief is incomplete. Physicians and nurses can help alleviate some of these emotions by proper care immediately after the loss and with appropriate follow-up but the bulk of support usually falls to the community members of the bereaved.

A major psychiatric text by Kaplan and Sadock explains that a multi-dimensional approach to helping the bereaved appears to be most successful. This approach includes education of the bereaved as to what to expect, encouraging expression of emotions, helping the bereaved come to terms with their new relationship with the deceased and helping the bereaved develop a new identity of his or her post-loss self.

For women who have suffered a pregnancy loss, education by professionals often consists of being told what to expect from their bodies. However, what to expect emotionally is not mentioned as frequently. Women need to know about the rollercoaster of emotions they will go through and about the different stages of mourning. They also need to know that eventually, they will feel better. Women and their partners often have questions they need to discuss about where their baby has gone, both physically and spiritually. They have a need to tell their story and hear the stories of others in order to have their feelings normalized and validated, rather than cloaked in silence and secrecy. This can be furthered through other couples' reaching out to help the grieving pair.

I want to make special mention of the needs of women who have had a pregnancy loss after infertility, as their grieving touches upon some special issues. The process of infertility treatment is physically grueling, emotionally demanding and financially draining. Many couples are anguished and fearful by the time a pregnancy is achieved. They are already grieving the loss of normal fertility. When they experience a pregnancy loss, they may, therefore, struggle mightily between hope for a future pregnancy and hopelessness for future fertility. Their anger and frustration may be heightened and they may feel that others cannot understand the despair and hopelessness they experience. They may be financially or emotionally unable to attempt another pregnancy and may need to grieve the loss of conceiving children.

It is time to break the silence and men and women have recognized the need to reach out to others at their time of loss. Hannah Stone has gathered stories that any grieving person can read at such a time. The men and women in these vignettes have all willingly spoken out in the hope of being able to help others through their storytelling. Our hope and the hope of these courageous couples is that through these stories, no one with a pregnancy loss need feel abandoned or alone.

Sources:

Adolfsson, Annsofie, Larsson P.G., Wijma, Barbro, Bertero, Carina (2004) Guilt and Emptiness: Women's Experiences of Miscarriage. *Health Care for Women International*, 25:543-560, 2004.

Kaplan, Harold I., Sadock, Benjamin J. *Comprehensive Textbook of Psychiatry*. 6th edition. Williams & Wilkins 1995.

Freda, Margaret Comerford, Devine, Kit S., Semelsberger, Carrie (2003) The Lived Experience of Miscarriage After Infertility. *MCN*, 28(1): 17-23, 2003.

Brier, Norman (1999) Understanding and Managing the Emotional Reactions to a Miscarriage. *Obstetrics and Gynecology*, 93 (1): 151-155.

Preface

For as long as I can remember, I have always wanted to be a mother.

As a little girl of three or four, I had imaginary friends who I talked to and bossed around as if they were my children. (I don't remember what I said but I do remember that they listened to my every word!) I also loved to play "house" with my "real" friends and of course in those scenarios, I was always the mommy.

As a teenager, my Saturday nights were spent babysitting. I'm sure that my friends wondered why I preferred playing Barbies with toddlers and pre-schoolers to a night out with "the gang." I guess I just enjoyed being around young children more than I did listening to the latest troubles plaguing my teenage friends. In my freshman year of high school, I decided I wanted to become a pediatrician. I volunteered at a local hospital one summer and spent a great deal of my "off" time in the pediatrics ward. I was determined to become the best pediatrician, combining my love of children with my love of medicine. What an interesting choice of profession, considering that I didn't like school very much and the very thought of four years of medical school was beyond me!

Well, I guess you have figured out from my lack of medical credentials that I never became a pediatrician. At 14, I had everything planned just perfectly – I was going to attend college in New York and then, Harvard Medical School. What I didn't plan on, however, was realizing at the mere age of 17 that I didn't want a career that would take me out of the house and away from my children. I knew that I wanted to marry "young" and I knew that I wanted to have a large family so going to medical school right after college and then going through a residency in pediatrics would not pan out. I never became "the best pediatrician." Instead, I became a writer. I am happy to report that I have fulfilled my life-long dream of becoming a mother. I have been blessed with a wonderful, supportive husband and five beautiful children who have given me nothing but joy.

Sadly, though, there have been some rough times in my journey through motherhood. In my quest for that "large" family, I have suffered three pregnancy losses. Each loss was devastating and a tremendous shock to my husband and me. There were family members and close friends to whom I could turn for comfort and a shoulder to cry on, yet I also felt that they really didn't want to hear me out. They would suggest to me that "it was for the best" or to be grateful that I had other children but somehow, that just didn't make me feel better.

At the time of each loss, I didn't know of any support groups in my area where I could meet and talk to other women. After my first miscarriage, I started to put my experience down on paper but then, I became pregnant with my oldest child. The "project" was postponed for nine months, with its author fully concentrated on having a healthy baby. Then, the "project" was postponed indefinitely as other "projects" piled up – baby #2, baby #3, baby # 4, baby # 5, potty training, pre-school, constant trips to the pediatrician, etc.

When I suffered my second miscarriage in 1997, I looked for any and all books that dealt with personal experiences of pregnancy loss. I came up with one book, written by a woman doctor who had suffered several miscarriages. Although hearing of her personal losses somewhat helped me through my own loss, I found all of the information on what can go wrong with a pregnancy both impersonal and depressing.

I wanted a book that would tell me that what I was feeling was normal and that I shouldn't feel the need to hide or be ashamed of my loss. After all, that is how I felt the people around me were making me feel. I needed a book that could help me say "the right things" to others who suffered similar losses…something other than, "I know what you're going through."

I never did find that book. And that is why I decided that nothing was going to stop me from finishing that "project." I hope that no other man or woman out there has to look that hard for a book again!

"Hannah"

It is Monday, February 28, 1994. I'm nearly 12 weeks along with my first pregnancy and today is the day that my husband and I are going to see our baby's heartbeat. I've never been so excited and terrified at the same time!

Up until now, I've been feeling great. I get tired once in a while but I've been spared the horrible morning sickness that has claimed most of my female relatives and friends. My husband thinks it's weird that I haven't been nauseous but I figure I'm just lucky.

Other than our parents and my grandfather, we haven't told anyone else yet since we want to get over that first trimester "danger zone." In fact, we only told my grandfather because he hasn't been feeling well and we know that the good news would make him feel better.

It's so hard to keep this news between us. We want to let my brother and sister-in-law know that their two-day-old daughter is going to be a big cousin in September. I know that it's only a matter of days before we make our announcement but I feel like I'm going to burst if I don't tell someone soon. When I went shopping for maternity clothes last week, I had to practically hide behind the clothes rack every time someone passed by the store for fear that I would be recognized and my secret would be out!

I just want this appointment to be over and done with already. I know everything is fine with the baby but I won't feel right until I see its heartbeat. Another sister-in-law of mine had a miscarriage a few months ago. She was about 12 weeks along in her pregnancy and when she went in to see her baby's heartbeat, she was told that there wasn't one. She had to have a D & C – she was absolutely devastated. She and I never discussed the miscarriage. I didn't know the right things to say or do. I couldn't imagine what it felt like to be in her shoes, having lost a part of her. I just knew that I never wanted to be in her shoes. Now that I'm pregnant, I'm sure that what happened to her is not going to happen to me. But until I see my baby moving on the ultrasound screen, I am going to worry.

G. is holding my hand and standing by my side in the examination room as my obstetrician enters. When she asks how I'm feeling, I tell her I feel fine but I'm nervous. I explain that my sister-in-law recently miscarried and I just want to leave this appointment, knowing that our baby is okay. With that said and done, she asks us if we want to see the baby's heartbeat. We don't need more than a second to tell her that we're ready.

It's hard for me to see anything since I'm lying down on the examination table but I can imagine everything the doctor is telling me. She sees the sac. Hooray! She moves the "wand" around but doesn't say much. After a moment or two, she cryptically says that she doesn't see anything inside. I'm nervous before she finishes her sentence but I feel better when she explains that the ultrasound equipment in her office isn't as reliable as that of radiologist. We are told to have an ultrasound done by the radiologist down the hall.

Before G. and I leave her office, the doctor hands me a pamphlet about a test that I'll be having at my next check-up that checks for abnormalities. I tell her I'll see her in a month.

When we get to the radiologist's office, we tell the receptionist that my doctor ordered an ultrasound for the fetal heartbeat. We're told that since it's already late in the day, we cannot be seen until 8:00 the next morning. With our appointment set, we go home with the knowledge that we'll be seeing our baby's heartbeat in less than 24 hours!

The next morning, G. and I drive separately to the radiologist's office since he'll be going to work immediately after the ultrasound is done. We're put in a room where I am told to lie down on the examination table and wait for the radiologist. When she arrives, we introduce ourselves and tell her that we're very excited about seeing the baby. G. holds my hand as we wait for the image of our baby to show up on the ultrasound screen. After a few minutes of moving the instrument around, the radiologist says that she doesn't see anything on the screen and asks us if we're sure of our conception date. Recalling that my last period was in December, we say yes, we're sure. Without offering an explanation, the radiologist tells us that she has to talk to my doctor.

Feeling that something is very wrong, G. presses her for an explanation. She coldly informs us that the fetus is not viable -- there is a sac but there is no heartbeat. She clarifies that while our baby should be almost 12 weeks gestation, it never developed a heartbeat or progressed with its development past eight weeks. I promptly burst into tears and mutter, "This cannot be happening." G., on the other hand, refuses to take the radiologist's word and demands that she repeat the ultrasound. She does, this time on my belly (the previous ultrasound was done vaginally), and confirms that our baby is dead.

Realizing that we need some time alone, the radiologist suggests that we go into her office and talk to my obstetrician, who is waiting for us on the telephone. (At some point during the ultrasound appointment, a call was placed to her office.) When I get on the line, the doctor says matter-of-factly that she's sorry about our loss and she informs me that I will have to undergo a D & C. Still in shock, I agree to wait until she returns from her vacation the following Tuesday to have the procedure done.

G. and I go down the hall to the doctor's office, where we are met by her nurse. The nurse extends her condolences and takes us into a private office where we can schedule the D & C. I am just so stunned by everything that has been happening that I let G. handle everything. When he asks the nurse if there is any way that I can have the D & C
done earlier, she responds that with my doctor being tied up in surgery all day today and then going on vacation, she will be unavailable until the following Tuesday.

Refusing to wait another seven days, G. demands that either my doctor performs the D & C today or he will personally find another doctor who will do it right away. The nurse calls the doctor at the hospital and gets her to agree to fit me in this afternoon. Once we go through the necessary insurance and pre-admitting procedures, we are told to report to the hospital at 11:30. My D & C is scheduled for 1:00 this afternoon.

We return to the radiologist's private office to collect the coats we had forgotten to take with us earlier and to start calling the family. G. calls my mother first. I just sit there in a state of shock as I hear him tell her about the miscarriage. Hearing him actually say "miscarriage" out loud makes me cry all over again. I get on the phone, tell her I will be okay and ask her to tell my father the news. Before hanging up, I promise to call her (it's only 8:30 at this point).

I can't bear to talk to her or to anyone else at this point. I feel like I'm having an out of body experience, watching all of this happening in front of me and feeling that there is nothing I, as a spectator, can do to change anything. Getting a hold of myself once again, I notice the radiologist walking a young man and woman out to the reception area. G. whispers to me that they were in the room next to us, having an ultrasound and they, too, were just told that their baby is dead.

Next, G. calls his mother, who is on vacation in Florida. As I take in everything that has been happening in the last 30 or 40 minutes, I hear him debating with his mother about whether or not I was as far along as I originally thought. This time, it's G. who is defending the radiologist. He assures his mother that we know I was almost 12 weeks along and that the baby's heart should have started to beat on its own by now.

G. tries to contact his father but he is told by his father's secretary that he will be in a meeting until later in the morning. With all of our calls to our parents made at this point, we realize that it's time to go home.

The car ride home is pure torture. Here, I thought I would be leaving my ultrasound appointment with pictures of our baby to show off. Instead, I'm going home with a piece of paper that will admit me to the hospital for a D & C that I do not want. I ask myself out loud, "What did I do wrong? Why is this happening to us?"

So many questions are going through my head. Did I sleep in the wrong position? Should I not have told my grandfather right away that I was pregnant? Did I eat the wrong food? Was the water that I was drinking full of toxins? Did I exercise too much? Had I been too worried about gaining too much weight with this pregnancy? I need an answer!

I'm in the car for about 30 seconds when G. phones to see if I'm okay. I tell him I will be okay and then I ask how he is holding up. I realize that this is not just happening to me. G. was just as excited about this baby as I was. I tell him that I love him. It's something I don't say often enough yet something I constantly feel. He tells me he loves me back. Before we know it, we're home.

To kill time, we decide to watch some television. We're sure the advertisers aren't aware of our situation but it seems as if every single commercial on television this morning has something to do with babies. There's a diaper commercial, an ad for baby formula, a 30 second spot on the latest Fisher Price toy. We're fine until an advertisement comes on with an ultrasound image of a ten week old fetus' heartbeat. The advertisement is for Pro-Life. The audience is asked how one can have an abortion at ten weeks once the fetus has already begun to live. As we watch this advertisement, we simultaneously wonder aloud, "Why would someone choose to terminate a pregnancy?" We aren't normally anti-abortion but on this morning, we most certainly are. Here, we're waiting for a procedure that is being called a "missed abortion," a term I despise. We aren't choosing to end this pregnancy…this pregnancy has been ended for us!

We flip through the various channels but nothing seems to hold our interest. Over the course of the next two hours or so, we hear from various friends and members of our family. My father-in-law finally returns our call and offers to be with G. during my D & C. He also volunteers to tell the rest of the family about our loss. (That is no problem for us, especially since we are in no mood to re-enact today's events with our siblings and extended family.)

Though G. assures his father that there is no need to come, I convince him to let his father keep him company. I don't want him to be alone if he doesn't have to be. I keep on reminding myself that G. is suffering just as much as I am and that waiting out my procedure with no one by his side is the last thing he needs.

My mother calls and tells us that she and my father are on their way to help us out when we come home from the hospital. I'm not sure how she can help us at this point in time. I remind her that my brother and sister-in-law need her more, what with a newborn daughter to take care of but she says she's coming. She says she wants to be with me right now. She then tells me that my grandfather wants to talk to me. I don't have more than a few seconds to steel myself for our conversation before he gets on the line. Zayda, as I call him, is crying but I assure him that G. and I are going to be okay. I tell him that I love him and that I will talk to him later. My mother gets back on the phone but we're interrupted by our call waiting so I tell her that I'll see her later this afternoon.

I don't remember who calls in what order but it seems as if everyone under the sun is calling us. My brother's wife calls and offers her condolences. Our call waiting ends our conversation and this time, it's my aunt.

My aunt and I have always been close so hearing from her means a lot. I am stunned when she confides to me that she, too, suffered a miscarriage. She tells me that it was also her first pregnancy and she had been about 11 or 12 weeks along when she miscarried. It's something that she hasn't shared with many people so knowing her "secret" eases my pain somewhat. And, hearing that she got pregnant with my cousin three months after her miscarriage gives me some hope that I, too, will become pregnant again quickly.

There is another call on the other line. At this point, we are wishing we had never heard of call waiting. All three of his brothers call, as do my two brothers. None of them really know what to say at this time except "I'm sorry."

I call another aunt so that she hears the news from me first. I have to choke back the tears as I tell her that I was planning to tell her some good news this week but that unfortunately, the good news is not so good anymore. She knows right away what I am trying to tell her and offers her sympathy.

I continue to receive calls from several friends who hear about our loss through the grapevine. They are all people who have suffered

13

one or more miscarriages. Two of my friends tell me that they got pregnant within three months after their miscarriages. I feel better hearing this but wonder if I will be able to get pregnant again so quickly. G. tells me not to even think about getting pregnant again. We need to concentrate right now on what will be happening in the next few hours.

Before we know it, it's time to leave for the hospital. It's so hard for me to believe that I won't be pregnant once I leave the hospital this afternoon. I know that the doctors have told me that my pregnancy really ended four weeks ago but I still feel pregnant. I don't feel any different now than I did last month or even last week. Walking through the hospital halls and corridors with G. holding my hand, I feel as if I'm walking to my own death sentencing. A very important part of me has died. I know I have no choice in what is happening to me. I just feel so numb and empty and tired. Why am I here?!

"I'm here for a D & C," I tell the receptionist. We're told that we've been pre-admitted by my doctor's office and that we should go upstairs. Upstairs, we are escorted by a nurse to a room at the end of the hall. I'm told to get undressed and to put on a hospital gown before getting into bed.

When I am given waiver forms to sign for the surgery and the anesthesiologist, I am told that I am authorizing the abortion of my fetus. Once again, this D & C is being referred to as an abortion. I hate that word! In my opinion, an abortion is a choice that a woman makes when it comes to whether or not she is going to continue a pregnancy. This is not something I am choosing to do. I would never, ever choose to abort any baby of mine. I know "abortion" is just a term but it's the wrong term in this situation. A nurse arrives to put in my I.V.

I'm all set for the D & C now. Another nurse and my doctor come into my room to take me into the operating room. I try to be brave as I kiss G. goodbye and tell him I love him and that I'll see him in a bit. I say goodbye to my father-in-law and tell him to take good care of G. while I'm gone. As I'm wheeled down the hall and taken to the elevator, I hear the sounds of crying babies. A woman in a wheelchair passes me by, holding her newborn baby. It suddenly dawns upon me that my room is on the postpartum floor. Granted, I was placed at the end of the hall but there are still new mothers and babies sharing the same floor as me!

14

Here I am, about to have my baby taken away from me and all I hear and see around me are new bouncing, healthy babies. It's just so heartless and insensitive of the hospital staff. For the last several hours, I've been grieving over the news that I am not going to be a mother so why am I being treated as a mother now? Couldn't I have been admitted to a surgical ward since I am being considered a surgical patient today?!

The operating room is very white, sterile and cold. I am moved onto a gurney and prepped for the D & C. My doctor arrives and tells me we're ready to start. A gas mask is placed over my nose and mouth as I am told to count from 100 to 0. I don't think I get to 90 before I succumb to the anesthesia.

When I open my eyes, I'm back in my room and find G. standing by my side. He asks me how I feel and I tell him I am so tired. All I want to do is sleep. Maybe if I sleep a little, this will prove to be a very bad dream and I will wake up pregnant again. I realize that it's not going to turn out that way when the doctor stops by my room to see how I'm feeling and to go over some recovery instructions with me. I am told not to take baths, swim or have sex until further notice. She tells me I can go home in a few hours, once the anesthesia wears off.

After she reminds me that she will be away for the next week, she says she'll see me in two weeks at my post-op appointment. When G. asks her if she knows anything more from the D & C about why I miscarried, she responds that the fetal tissue has been sent off to the pathology lab but it's too soon to tell. I groggily ask her if I did anything wrong to make this miscarriage happen. She replies, "No," and explains that one in every four pregnancies results in a miscarriage.

"It shouldn't happen to you again," she says before saying goodbye. It shouldn't have happened at all, I think to myself. I sleep on and off for the next hour or so.

Even though I still feel tired, I am eager to go home. I want nothing more than to get into my own bed and a comfortable one, at that! A nurse takes my blood pressure one more time and gets my discharge papers in order.

At home, I get undressed and into bed. G. joins me upstairs and reports that there were several messages on our answering machine. Several of our friends have called to express their condolences, having heard the bad news through today's grapevine. There is a message from my parents, telling us that they should be at our house by 6:30. My aunt also called to tell us that she will be bringing dinner over for us tonight.

I'm feeling somewhat better now. I don't feel as tired, now that the anesthesia has worn off. I also feel as if I don't have any more tears to shed. It finally hits me that I am no longer pregnant when I go to the bathroom and see my soiled sanitary pads. I feel so dirty and impure…not just from the blood but from realizing what I have experienced today.

Getting back into bed, I ask myself why God would allow this to happen. Why would He answer my prayers to become pregnant, only to have me miscarry? Why couldn't I just go on "un-pregnant" for another three months instead of going through this torture? I have always had a strong belief in God. I have never lost my faith in Him, even when things have gone wrong. Why would He turn his back on me now?

Needing answers, I call a friend whom I consider to be my spiritual advisor. He tells me that we cannot question why God does the things that He does. Yes, it's unfair that I had to lose a baby I so desperately wanted but I can't lose faith now. There is a reason for everything; we may not know the reason for the miscarriage right now but someday, we will.

I keep a brave front when my parents arrive. We never actually discuss the miscarriage or how G. and I are feeling. At this point, I just want to move on with our lives. It isn't until the next morning, when I wake up and come to grips with what has happened in the past 24 hours. Breaking down in G.'s arms, I say over and over again, "It isn't fair!" My mother must have heard me down the hall because she is at my side within seconds and crying along with us.

Once my parents leave, I realize that it's time to move on. G. returns to work on Thursday but calls me practically every hour on the hour to see how I am doing. I always tell him, "I'm fine. How are you?" He always answers, "Doing better but it's not easy." My mother-in-law calls from Florida and asks me if I will go to lunch with her on Friday. She says she will be back home tonight and would really like to spend some time with me before G. and I leave town for the weekend. Although I'm really not in the mood to go out in public at this point, I decide to go. I just worry that people will look at me and know right away what has happened to me. I know people didn't know beforehand that I was pregnant but word has gotten around about my miscarriage.

My mother-in-law and I don't really discuss the miscarriage during our outing; in fact, we try to talk about anything but the miscarriage. It's not until we're on the way home and a block away from my house that she says that she feels bad that she wasn't there for us on Tuesday. I assure her that we don't blame her. It's not as if she knew this was going to happen. We get all teary as she takes my hand and tells me that I am handling this so well. I answer that I wish I didn't have to handle this at all.

Returning to my doctor's office for a post-operative check-up two weeks later, I am filled with mixed emotions. I am sad, coming to see her for what should have been my 16 week pre-natal check-up. I am also relieved, knowing that the worst is over and that I am moving on with my life. My doctor once again assures me that I did nothing to make this miscarriage happen. It was just "bad luck" and that unfortunately, miscarriages do happen. I do feel better when she tells me that there is no reason why I should miscarry again. Once she is finished examining me, she tells me that I am doing fine and that I can try to get pregnant again after two full menstrual cycles.

Life proves to go on. I pour myself into my work and I try not to think about everyone around me who is either delivering babies or announcing that they are pregnant. It seems as if there is something in the water…I just need to wait to have my cup!

More and more people in the community find out that I had been pregnant yet no one wants to talk about it. It's as if they are either trying to avoid the subject or they are trying to actually forget that it ever happened. I know people get uncomfortable when it comes to the topic of miscarriage. I admit that I was nervous about approaching one of my closest female friends when she went through a miscarriage but I knew that ignoring it isn't the answer. I don't want people who are close to me to feel that they have to turn the other way when I walk into a room or never mention the word "pregnant" around me again. This makes me feel as if I have to keep my miscarriage experience to myself…that it is something I can never talk about with anyone other than G.

I take on as many projects at work as possible and in my free time, I start a journal in which I write about my miscarriage experience. I don't tell anyone, not even G., that I am doing this. It's my secret. It's my time to think about the baby we lost. Even though I feel a little bit better each day that passes by, I still feel the need to express my emotions. I know in my heart that this pain is something that will never go away. It will get easier as time goes by but it will never go away.

We are invited to celebrate Mothers' Day at his parents' house. Everyone is exchanging cards as we arrive. We are all smiles as we hand out our cards to all of the women in the family, yet neither of us is hardly happy on the inside. This was supposed to be my first Mother's Day as a mother-to-be! I should be receiving good wishes and Mother's Day cards, along with my mother-in-law, sister-in-law and G.'s grandmother! When I first found out I was pregnant, I had so been looking forward to celebrating my first Mother's Day with a baby growing inside of me. I can't help but feel cheated right now. Hopefully, G. will be able to celebrate this Father's Day as a newly discovered father-to-be.

Unfortunately, there aren't any Father's Day cards to give to G. this year after all. I won't lie and say that I'm not sad when I get my period in the beginning of June. What makes it worse is that I keep hearing my friends' voices in my head telling me, "I got pregnant two months after my miscarriage," or "You'll see. You'll get pregnant right away because your body is so ripe." I remind myself that it took me a few months to get pregnant the first time so it's more likely that it will take me a few months this time. I want to get pregnant so badly…it actually hurts. It's not as if I'm trying to replace the baby we lost. I just want to be able to hold a baby in my arms…a baby to call my own. I want to be able to hear someone call me "Mommy." I want to feel the same unconditional love that my friends share with their kids. I don't want to wait another month!

Another month goes by and I get my period on July 2. I start to worry that I won't be able to conceive again. I start to think about all of my friends who had to turn to fertility specialists in order to have their babies. Will I have to go through the same heartache they did? What if the miscarriage was God's way of telling me that I only had one chance to become a mother and I blew it? I call my friend (the spiritual advisor,

I call him) and share my doubts with him. He encourages me to be patient since I didn't get pregnant overnight last time. Reminding me to "keep the faith," he says he's sure that he'll be hearing some good news from me very soon.

"Leann"

On August 16, 2004, Logan's father, Chris, and I found out we were pregnant. We were both 18 and scared to death. After the initial shock wore off, we both became excited about the baby. A couple of weeks later, Chris went on tour with Avalon and Mark Schultz to do the lighting and sound. He was so excited. He told all the other crew guys about the baby. They teased him about getting him a diaper genie because according to them, you can't have a baby and not have a diaper genie!

On September 27, I went to my first appointment with the doctor. He told me how good the baby looked and how active the baby was. Our due date was to be April 6, 2005. While Chris was on tour, my mom, my sisters and I began to plan for the baby and the nursery. It was going to be done in Baby Snoopy. I was so excited about my baby. I couldn't wait until April to hold and see him for the first time.

My pregnancy was going extremely well. I didn't even have morning sickness.

On November 16, I went in for my official ultrasound to find out what the baby was. The technician told me how good the baby looked and that it was a boy. He moved his due date to April 2 and said again that the baby looked good and was extremely active. I was so excited when the technician told me it was a boy. I immediately called Chris and told him. He, too, was ecstatic because a boy is what he really wanted.

Chris came home off tour a week later and we had Thanksgiving together. Everything was going well and I was getting big.

Then, that Monday, I went in for my monthly check-up. My blood pressure was really high so my doctor decided to run some blood work and then told me to come back on Wednesday. Thinking it was just a fluke, Chris and I went to a hockey game the next night and we had a lot of fun.

On Wednesday, December 1, my whole world turned upside down. I went into the doctor's office and my blood pressure was still really high. My doctor explained to me that he thought I was developing Pre-Eclampsia. (Being that I was only 23 weeks along, it was way too early for me to be getting it.) The doctor did what he thought was best and called a high risk doctor in Tulsa, which is an hour away. I was admitted to a hospital in Tulsa that evening to find out exactly what was going on.

I began to feel scared but at the same time, I thought I was just going in for a few tests. I figured they would find out what was wrong, fix it and I would go home in a couple of days to finish out my pregnancy. I thought at the very worst, I would be on bed rest until April. (After all, Logan's heartbeat still sounded great.)

After a very restless night, I was wheeled on a stretcher down to radiology for an ultrasound. That was when they told me that some time in the last 12 hours, my baby had died. I was devastated. All I can remember is sitting there in complete shock and seeing our baby on the screen, not moving or anything. They wheeled me back upstairs and said the doctor would be in after a while to discuss where we were going to go from there.

After what seemed like an eternity, I got in touch with my mom and Chris by phone. They immediately rushed back to the hospital. The doctor came in and explained that since I was 23 weeks along, he would have to induce my labor. I would have to give birth as if I was delivering a perfectly healthy baby. To me, that just didn't seem fair. I knew it wasn't the doctor's fault but I just couldn't understand why I had to go through that, knowing there wasn't a reward at the end. My baby would never cry, never laugh, never breath. I was too sick for them to be able to

21

send me home and at that point, I was on complete bed rest because of the Pre-Eclampsia.

They began to induce my labor that night. I was still in complete shock. The nurses came in with bereavement material and recommended that we name the baby. They explained that we would need to designate a funeral home to pick up the baby when I was released from the hospital.

Still in shock, I went on with my labor. On December 3, I delivered our baby boy at 10:35 P.M. He was absolutely perfect. We named him Logan Michael. Chris decided on naming him after a drummer from Avalon when we found out it was a boy. My sisters and Chris' sister came up to the hospital to hold Logan. The next day was my twin sister's and my birthday. We celebrated it at the hospital and held Logan and loved him some more. I wanted to hold him all I could before I left. My mom had talked me into seeing him in the first place because I was initially afraid of what he would look like.

On Sunday evening, I finally got to go home. Much to my surprise, I found myself not wanting to leave the hospital because I knew I was leaving empty handed. On Monday, we made the funeral arrangements. The funeral home went to Tulsa to get Logan. They did everything, including going to get him for no charge.

I spent the whole week in a daze. We had Logan's funeral on December 10. Things didn't really hit me until the next day.

Since then, life has been a roller coaster of emotions. Sadly, Chris and I have parted and a friendship of 10 years is gone. Some time in January, he simply looked at me and said we could no longer be together because Logan had died.

I miss my baby boy more than anything in the world. I've gotten through Christmas, Easter and his due date. Things are hard, really hard…like a roller coaster of emotions. Eventually, the raw feeling will go away. Until then, I take comfort knowing that I will get to see and hold my baby one day and then, it will be forever. God is taking care of him until I can get there to do it.

For some reason, Logan was needed in heaven more than he was needed here. That doesn't take the pain away but it helps me to cope in knowing that our parting is just temporary. I will always cherish the moments I got to hold Logan and I have kept everything of his that I could, including his clothes from the hospital, his receiving blanket, his pictures, etc. He was here for a short time but he managed to bring out both the worst and the best in the people around him. He taught me more about life than anyone else ever has or ever will. He will always be loved and missed.

"Dan"

Part 1

Caitlyn was over a year old and while still having some sleep problems, we were making progress on solving them. Tara and I had always planned on two children, and we wanted them about two years apart. So when we got back from our summer visit back east, we figured it was time to start working on another child. We conceived in early September and within a few days, Tara felt something was "different." So then we had to wait. When Tara missed her next period, we ran out and got a home pregnancy test and sure enough, it confirmed the good news.

My brother and his wife called their second child "sib" (short for sibling) while in utero. We thought that was really cute, but we couldn't use that name because it had been taken. We searched on the Internet for "two" in other languages, and eventually settled on the Swahili word Mbili. So that was the baby's in utero name.

As far as a name for the baby when born, we decided on Douglas Griffin for a boy and Keena for a girl. We didn't want to know if it was a boy or girl so we picked out both sets. Unfortunately, we never decided ahead of time on a second middle name if she was a girl.

The first months of the pregnancy were pretty normal. Psychologically, we were ready for this child and very much looking forward to welcoming him/her into our family. When Tara asked Cailyn "where is the baby?" Cailyn would usually come over, lift up Tara's shirt and pat her tummy.

Tara's cravings during month two were lasagna and cheese whiz (icky! We'd pretty much banned that vile stuff from the house but you can't argue with a pregnant woman's cravings.) During the third month, Tara craved fries and eggs.

Meanwhile, our family doctor who oversaw our first pregnancy had decided to get out of maternity. So instead of finding another doctor, we went with a midwife. The different outlook and type of care provided by a midwife sat really well with us.

At the 13 week visit to the mid-wife on November 27, Tara heard the heartbeat over the Doppler monitor. I'd wanted to be there to record it like I'd done with Cailyn. Unfortunately, Cailyn was getting into things in the office so I took her out to walk around and play. I'd hoped that they would call me when they were listening for the heartbeat but they were running a little late. At the time, I was a little sad that I missed it. I thought, 'big deal. I'll record it next time.' Little did we know that would be the last time we would hear Mbili's heartbeat.

By this time, Tara was feeling much better, and she was very hungry all of the time. The nausea she had felt for months had tapered off and Cailyn was sleeping much better. Everyone was feeling rested. Tara was also starting to feel what she thought to be movements.

The 16 week visit was Thursday, December 18 and included a complete examination so Cailyn and I stayed out in the clinic waiting room. Midway through the examination, they tried to hear the heartbeat again with the Doppler monitor. For some reason, the monitor was really scratchy and fuzzy, and it couldn't pick up the heartbeat. We figured that the monitor was having problems and maybe Mbili was in an awkward place. The midwife offered us the opportunity for an ultrasound to confirm things but we weren't worried. Indeed, we had to go for an ultrasound two weeks later anyway so we thought that we could wait rather than subject Mbili to two ultrasounds in a short time frame.

The following Sunday, we had a Christmas party. It was December 21. As with most Christmas parties, the food we ate wasn't the greatest – chips, jalapeno peppers, chocolates, etc. On Monday morning, December 22, Tara woke up with some cramping and a little spotting. I had tummy cramps too so we figured that was due to the food. The spotting was a little more worrisome. We thought perhaps, it was still related to the Pap smear done on the previous Thursday. Nonetheless, we decided to check with the mid-wife. By this point, she was over in Vancouver and someone else was filling in for her. That midwife thought we should come over for a check. Her Doppler monitor was not fuzzy but she couldn't find a heartbeat either. Still, that was not definitive and we arranged for an ultrasound for us that afternoon.

The ultrasound showed that Mbili had died. There was no heartbeat. The ultrasound technician was very compassionate but there wasn't much she could do to sugarcoat the news. The ultrasound dated Mbili at 12 weeks and five days. We know we'd heard her heartbeat at 13 weeks. Our theory is that Mbili had been growing slower than normal and perhaps, that was why she died.

On December 23, Tara had actually felt some light contractions starting. We weren't ready emotionally for Mbili to be born and we wanted her birth to be special. Tara asked Mbili to wait until after Christmas. She wanted Cailyn to have a somewhat normal Christmas and for Mbili to still be safe and protected inside Mommy.

On Wednesday, December 24, we went into the hospital to talk to the doctor. We had three options, one of which he didn't overly recommend. First, we could have a D & C operation to remove Mbili but the soonest they could schedule one was midnight that night (Christmas Eve). That would have ruined Cailyn's Christmas so we said no. The second option was to take a drug to induce contractions -- Misoprostol. We did some research on that drug and we weren't particularly thrilled with it. The third option was to wait until nature took its course. The doctor wasn't overly pleased with this course of action, mainly over a concern of how long Mbili had actually been dead. So when we returned from the doctor's, we discussed the options between us, and then with the midwife. We decided to let things run their course – no interventions yet.

By December 27, we were starting to get a little emotionally drained by this. We'd managed to have a good Christmas with Cailyn. Tara and I had talked lots and we had pretty much come to grips with what was happening. We talked with the midwife, who presented us with a couple of choices of herbal concoctions. We opted for the castor oil. I always thought it was a laxative (and not that it could induce labor).

Tara took it late in the afternoon and the contractions started in the evening. They were very light. Then from 2:00 A.M. until 6:00 A.M., they were quite strong. Then, they stopped. We discussed this with the midwife, and she suggested we take another dose of the castor oil, which Tara did. Nothing happened. We figured that Tara's body knew that Cailyn was up and active during the day and she wouldn't let the contractions happen.

The doctor then called the midwife, saying that we really needed to get the baby out. He was getting concerned. We waited the rest of the day and talked with the midwife some more about the risks of taking the Misoprostol.

On the afternoon of the next day (by now December 30), we decided to try the Misoprostol. Tara took it and then we went for an evening walk around Buchart Gardens to look at the lights. A part of the way through the walk, Tara could feel light contractions starting. We got home and put Cailyn to bed. Tara wanted to labor in peace and I was "hovering" so I went to bed. I figured my primary job was to keep Cailyn occupied and out of the way. It was about 10:00 P.M.

At midnight, I woke up and went to check with Tara. She was in the living room on her exercise ball. I immediately got concerned as she seemed to be in a lot of pain. I didn't think I really liked the birthing process. I found it very difficult to sit calmly and watch someone I cared about going through intense pain during the contractions. I helped Tara prepare a bath and that was where she labored until Mbili was born. Around 1:30, the concern got too much for me and I phoned our midwife. We discussed things for a bit and she told me just to sit with Tara and see how things go.

At 2:30, still frantic, I called the mid-wife again and together, we thought that perhaps, Tara was getting close and the mid-wife would come over. Tara hadn't really wanted to call because she was concerned about imposing upon the mid-wife. Once she got here, both Tara and I were a lot more relaxed. The mid-wife didn't "do" anything beyond sitting with us in the bathroom and talking with us but just her doing that was awesome. It helped enormously. I was calmer because she was someone who'd seen births before and knew the process while, despite having taken the pre-natal course and read a number of books, I was finding the process very unnerving. Tara was finding the contractions very tiring. During the half-hour or so it took the midwife to show up, Tara told me that for our next child, I should be sure to book the C-section early.

Just before 4:00 A.M., the contractions were slowing down. Tara was exhausted, and she wanted the process to be over. She was nearly at her limit. As she put it later, "if there had been an off switch, I'd have used it and given up." She'd been going through over 10 hours of labor, seven plus hours of which were very intense. That is the problem with the Misoprostol (or many other interventions). Unlike normal drug-free labor which slowly builds, Tara's labor went pretty quickly to the intense phase of contractions and stayed there. No wonder so many mothers want heavy duty pain killer drugs!

The three of us were discussing the contraction slowdown, and what that meant. The midwife was concerned that it meant the drug was wearing off and the birth might not happen. If Tara didn't take another pill, then all of her labor to date would've been for nothing and we'd have to start again. Tara, on the other hand, wasn't mentally able to face another six plus hours of labor like the hours she'd been through. She wanted it to be over. We briefly discussed the D & C option. At this point, Cailyn started to stir so I had to get up and get her back to sleep.

I came back and Tara and the midwife had pretty much decided to check Tara's cervix to see how dilated she was. We would make a decision based on that. Then suddenly, there were two very strong contractions that came one after the other and Tara had the strong desire to push. Incidentally, earlier in the evening, Tara had asked the midwife, "How will I know when it is time to push?" "You will know." "Really?" "Yeah, really." Talking about it afterwards, Tara said that when the urge comes to push, you do know. There is no doubt.

Tara felt a bit of panic at that moment but then Mbili came out, still in her sac. The midwife caught her in a wet piece of green linen she'd brought. It was 4:30 A.M., December 31.

Tara put down her thoughts in an e-mail to her mom a little later, and I think those words nicely describe what happened.

"…she was still safe in her sac and it really was a beautiful and peaceful sight to see her all nicely protected in what has been her home all along. We decided to keep her in her safe haven. I did get to look at her through the sac and see her little arms and legs. She was also much smaller than the ultrasound last week showed so she has been shrinking.

All in all, it was a pretty peaceful and amazing birth. Of course, minus the outcome. The actual birthing process was what I had wanted with Cailyn and I felt quite good and at peace with the whole thing. Because she was still in her sac, we know everything came out and the after bleeding has been non-existent to minimal. The mid-wife was quite shocked at how easy it went.

Well, I am off to bed. I am exhausted, but I feel even more at peace with everything."

Tara (written at about 5:15 A.M.)

We buried Keena Mbili in the afternoon of January 1. On the afternoon of December 31, we'd gone to a local plant nursery and gotten a dwarf Alberta spruce that was about 1.5 feet tall. They are not supposed to get much more than six to eight feet tall so it would fit nicely in the front.

We buried Mbili still in her sac and still wrapped in the green linen cloth with a short ceremony with just Tara, myself, Cailyn and my dad present. My dad read a few passages from the Anglican prayer book. It was both incredibly sad and strangely peaceful to bury her. Then we planted the tree to commemorate her. Every Christmas, we will decorate her tree with lights to remember her.

On January 3, it snowed and it blanketed her tree. It was beautiful.

Part II

After the loss of our daughter, Keena, in December of 2003, we were anxious to try again. By the end of March, my wife, Tara, was feeling good so we decided to try again quickly. In early April, Tara felt pregnant again. We used the second of the pregnancy tests we'd brought for Keena and it confirmed the good news. The expected due date was December 28, which seemed very fitting after the loss of Keena.

We looked around for a good name for "three" but nothing struck our fancy. Then, one of Tara's online friends remarked that because this one was due near Christmas, Mistletoe might be appropriate. This became our in-utero name, but it didn't seem quite right to include that in Faolan's formal name. (We never managed to find suitable names for the child until the last two weeks. At that point, we noticed Faolan meant "little wolf" or "little spirit wolf." That seemed appropriate.

We didn't relax until we passed the 16 week threshold, when we had learned that Keena was dead. We kept the news of our pregnancy relatively quiet. We were doing bi-weekly visits with our midwife and because we were going back east for a month, we arranged with a midwife in Kingston to have a quick check-up and listen for the fetal heart beat for the 14th week check-up. Everything was fine. In hindsight, I think we were too fixated on the fetal heartbeat and thought that as long as we had "that," everything would be fine.

During the check-up in Kingston, it took the midwife a few minutes to find the heartbeat and as the time stretched out, Tara and I looked at each other silently saying, "oh no, not again" to each other. Then when she got the heartbeat, we both felt a great sigh of relief.

We decided to go with Jules Atkins as the midwife for this pregnancy. She was the lady who came over and helped us through Keena's miscarriage. We felt she had gone above and beyond the call of duty on that event so we wanted her to work with us on what we hoped would be a normal pregnancy. True to form, we found Jules was a superb midwife and once again, she went far above what we expected.

We thought everything was doing so well and then we went for the 20 week ultrasound. It was August 5.

The technician was quiet while she worked through the scan. Then she asked us to wait when she called the doctor in. This is never a good sign. The doctor took a look at the scans and told us that they were very concerned about a very low level of amniotic fluid. The baby appeared to be about two weeks smaller than he/she should have been. He recommended that we have another ultrasound done by a specialist. We went home a little concerned and did a pile of research. In many cases, the fluid levels replenished themselves and the pregnancies carried on with successful outcomes. We also thought that Tara might've been a little dehydrated – she hadn't been drinking much water and we'd been having a very hot (for Vancouver Island) stretch of weather. Tara drank nearly six liters of water that evening and then continued to drink a lot of water every day.

On August 10, Tara felt the first real movements of the baby. Up until then, there had only been "fluttering." On the following day, there was a good four hour period of strong movement. This raised our hopes that this was just a temporary aberration and that things were returning to normal.

Our midwife got us an appointment with the head of the neo-natal department of the Victoria General Hospital, Dr. Jerome Dansereau. The appointment was for the next Friday, ironically, Friday the 13th. We were very impressed with Dr. Dansereau. He did his own ultrasound scan. First he asked us to be quiet as he looked at everything. He then came back and discussed his findings and showed us what he was talking about on the monitor. He spent a lot of time with us. There were problems.

His biggest concern was the lack of amniotic fluid. Tara's increased water intake hadn't made a difference. Not only does the amniotic fluid provide a safety cushion for the baby against bumps and jars from the outside world, but it plays a crucial role in lung development. Without sufficient amniotic fluid, a baby's lungs will not develop.

Other issues he saw included swelling and fluid retention in the baby's head and neck area, only one visible kidney. The pictures of the baby's kidney area indicated the possibility of kidney damage, no bladder, a bright spot on the heart and a fluid filled area in the brain. He

31

stressed that both the second kidney and the bladder might be there. A lot of these issues by themselves were not cause to worry but taken together, they indicated that something was abnormal with the baby. He was concerned that we may have a Downs' baby – and a "bad" Downs' baby with life threatening problems. He suggested we do an amniocentesis. Normally, we are against these as they pose a measurable risk to the fetus plus they involve a long needle inserted into one's abdomen. We said we would think about it but we would like to wait a few weeks to see if things get better or not.

We were very impressed with Dr. Dansereau's willingness to explain things and to tell us why he was thinking certain ways. He didn't take the "I am the doctor and I've gone to school for X years and I know everything" approach. And he was very compassionate.

Our next appointment was August 26. We were "so" hoping that things would have taken a turn for the better. They hadn't. There was even less amniotic fluid than before. This time, though, they could see both kidneys and the bladder, but both kidneys were still discolored, indicating some sort of damage was occurring/continuing.

Tara and I thought about it and agreed to try an amnio – it would be able to definitively say whether our little child had a genetic disorder. Unfortunately, there was not enough fluid to get a proper sample. Usually, they like to draw 20 cc.'s but could make do with 10 cc.'s and maybe in an emergency, they could work with five. They got one cc. and that got contaminated with blood when they tried to move the needle to find some more. And the moving was extremely uncomfortable for Tara. So we had to give up on the amnio. Incidentally, Dr. Dansereau also did the amnio, with help from an ultrasound technician and a nursing assistant.

After the failed amnio, we discussed our options with Dr. Dansereau. He said that there was still a 90-95% chance of getting this information if they get the baby within a week of its dying. So that it is likely the route we will take to answer the question of chromosomal problems.

We went home and thought about the poor child. If things did not get better, then there was little hope (1% and that was being generous) that the child would live even if he survived to term. The amount of amniotic fluid was continuing to be reduced and Tara was sure she could feel the baby's head with her hand very clearly. He was obviously not being protected and we found that very scary. It was a tough couple of days.

On Monday, August 29, we called Jules and asked her to set up a meeting with Dr. Dansereau as soon as possible. It seemed pointless to continue if things were getting worse, plus at this point, the child could be starting to experience pain. Without the amniotic fluid to cushion him, every bump that Tara was getting (including being climbed on by Cailyn) was being transferred to the baby. It seemed cruel to continue and it seemed cruel to Cailyn to cringe whenever she came near Momma.

However, we did not want to terminate the pregnancy without one last ultrasound to confirm that things were still as bleak.

We were a bit surprised at how fast an appointment was set up – that Wednesday, September 1.

And wouldn't you know it? Things "were" better. There was more amniotic fluid (still way down from normal, but this was the first time we saw a reversal in the downward trend). The fluid retention and swelling on the child were down and the kidneys appeared to be a little less "abnormal." There would now be a change in plans. Perhaps this was a temporary thing – possibly a virus – and we were seeing the start of the recovery. At this point, Dr. Dansereau candidly told us that we should not get our hopes up but he thought that we might have a 5-10% chance of a successful pregnancy "IF" we didn't have any chromosomal problems. At best, he thought there was a 50-50 chance of chromosome problems.

Tara and I discussed things again and we decided to try the amnio again. An amnio would rule out or confirm the chromosome problem. Dr. Dansereau quickly arranged a team and they managed to withdraw 10 cc's of fluid. The results could take up to two weeks to come back. But we left the hospital with the first bit of good news in four weeks. We had another consultation set up with Dr. Dansereau on September 14.

On Wednesday, my brother's wife, Joanne, and her two children came down. They were under the impression that we would be inducing labor and had come down to help care for Cailyn and assist Tara and myself during this rough period. They also brought back Grandpa, who had been stuck in Castelgar, waiting for decent weather to ferry FWUN back to the coast. With the change in plans, Jo didn't have to look after anyone, other than normal mothering. We took the opportunity to have Cailyn meet and play with her cousins for a few days. Joanne, the kids and Grandpa left on the following Wednesday and Grandpa was able to fly back on Friday.

We met with Jules on September 8 for our weekly check-up and she mentioned that she had been discussing our case with a doctor. He had asked if anyone had considered "Parva Virus." We stopped off at the Sidney clinic and Tara had some blood taken and sent to the lab to see if she had any indications of having been exposed to that virus in the last couple of months. Then we went home to research on the net. And sure enough, exposure to this virus is commonly misdiagnosed as a chromosomal disorder and it can cause significantly reduced amniotic fluid levels. There is no lasting damage and things do get better. Things were continuing to look up.

Thursday was Tara's birthday. That evening, Tara and I were talking together, and I was able to feel our little baby kick a few times.

On Friday, Jules called to tell us that the results from the amniotic tests were in. Everything crashed down.

Our child had an extremely rare chromosome problem called "Trisomy 9." There were less than 30 documented cases in the medical literature worldwide since its discovery/identification in 1973. There are two variations – "mosaic," where not all the cells have it, and "complete," where all cells have the chromosome problems. There are a few mosaic babies that have survived, but with significant problems. Complete Trisomy 9 is completely lethal; if babies survive to birth, they live minutes. Indeed, most babies with the complete version die long before they reach 24 weeks. Of course, our baby had complete Trisomy 9.

We had a rather depressing weekend. We really didn't have much of a decision to make. Even if we managed to keep the baby alive until he was born at term, he (or she) would die within minutes. As bad as the news was, we now had a definitive answer and there was no more wondering whether the baby would recover from this.

Our next appointment with Dr. Dansereau was on Tuesday, September 14. Originally, we were to go over to medical imaging for a full scan; this was assuming that the chromosomes were okay and then he would want to ensure that there were no lasting internal problems. With the results indicating that we had a major chromosomal problem, the scan was unnecessary and we just met with Dr. Dansereau.

He gave us a couple of Misoprostol tablets. Unlike the doctor at Christmas, Dr. Dansereau was concerned about the possibility of uterine rupture (after the C-section Tara had with Cailyn). He advised us to take only 50 mg. (1/4 tablet) intra-vaginally every 12 hours, as opposed to 200 mg. orally every six to eight hours. He hoped that labor would start off easier and that within a day or so, Tara would be in full labor. He wanted to see us on Thursday morning if nothing was happening.

So that night, at about 8:30 P.M., Tara took the first dose. She got a few minor contractions, but more cramping. The next morning and then again that evening, she took the next dosages. The contractions came and went and the cramping was equivalent to a bad menstrual cramp.

On Thursday morning, we met again with Dr. Dansereau. We didn't do another Misoprostol dose beforehand in case he wanted to change the amount. He didn't. He was satisfied with the progress we were having, albeit slow. He gave Tara another pill and admonished us to be sure to go to the hospital once the contractions were happening. He didn't want us laboring at home.

On Thursday afternoon, Tara, Cailyn and I went to Buchart Gardens and walked around the flowers. It was a nice way to relax and prepare for what was coming, plus they say walking helps get labor going. We picked up some Thai food from a local restaurant and had that for dinner. Throughout the day, Tara was feeling contractions ranging from three's to five's on a scale of one to ten.

The contractions continued overnight. In the morning, they strengthened. At 8:30 A.M., Tara came out and said that if the contractions continued for the next 45 minutes, then we would probably head to the hospital. I called and left a message for Jules, telling her that we might be heading in soon.

At 9:30, Tara got up and said it was time. She was experiencing consistent "fives" every couple of minutes and they hadn't let up. They were not excruciating but they caused her to stop what she was doing and concentrate to ride them through. We left Cailyn with Grandpa and headed to the hospital.

The weather was gorgeous – this was the first blue sky day in a week or longer. It was kind of ironic yet calming and strengthening as well. We got to the hospital and up to our room by about 11:00 A.M. There was a special private room set aside for us in the ante-natal wing. The hospital was really great. Jules was already there. Tara had labored unmedicated with Keena at Christmas so she knew she could do it. With this birth though, we were already so emotionally tired after the six weeks of up and down, hope and no hope roller coaster, that she was feeling a bit of an "I don't care anymore" attitude. She thought that she would accept some pain relief medication. We opted for Phentol. An epidural was out of the question and the other option was one of the opiates like Demerol. I have to admit, I was happier seeing Tara taking something for the pain. I know she is the one actually dealing with the pain and I have no right to interfere but I feel so damn useless watching the one I love, in pain when there is nothing I can do about it. (After having observed labor twice now, I have to admit I am not a big fan of it).

The drugs took the edge off the contractions but as the day wore on, they did less and less. As Tara put it, they moved the pain down from a 10 to a nine – not a big difference. What they did do though, was slow the onset and speed the release of the contractions so that Tara got a bit more time in between the contractions.

Jules used her Doppler monitor to check for the baby's heartbeat – there was no heartbeat. Tara was not surprised. Jules asked us if we knew the sex of the baby. We said no but Tara was sure it was a boy. Jules said she was right. As far as knowing Faolan was already dead, I think that helped. Both Tara and I were concerned how he would've felt during the labor and birth had he been alive, and whether that would've caused him pain. So we took some solace in knowing he died in a warm and relatively safe place.

For the next six hours, Tara went through labor and I tried to help, which was mainly doing nothing and then reassure her during the breaks. She did NOT want to be touched during the contractions. And all those breathing exercises they talk about at prenatal classes? I think those are for the father, not the mother. Jules was watching everything carefully and assisting where she could but this was something that Tara had to do.

In the late afternoon, Tara's water broke and she moved into more of a kneeling position. I moved around and was able to hold and support her through the contractions – at least I was doing something useful now. Faolan was breech and his feet came out first. The birthing was pretty hard, as Tara was pretty tired. During the hardest part, I silently called to the spirits of Faolan, Keena and my mother to help Tara and give her strength.

Eventually at 5:14 P.M., Faolan was born. He was so tiny, and was pretty badly bruised. Looking at him, it was easy that things were not completely right. Still, he was our child and it was a very sad time. Jules and the nurse discreetly left the room to leave us alone with Faolan. I took a few pictures so that we can keep them in memory.

We hadn't done this with Keena and we have regretted it since. After about 10 minutes, I left Tara alone with him. We'd talked about this earlier – she wanted some time alone with him. By that point, Tara had already said her goodbyes and wanted only to rest and sleep. I filled in a few forms (gotta love that paperwork!), authorizing an autopsy to be performed. We didn't need the results, but perhaps something can be learned by the scientific community. If so, then Faolan's death would at least have had some good outcome. Then Jules and I went back in to see Tara.

I held Faolan while Tara birthed the afterbirth, then we gently put Faolan down on the other bed in the room. That was the last time we held or saw him. Jules took him out to weigh him and then to try to get some foot prints. We'd brought a plaster footprint kit with us but Jules kindly advised against trying it. Faolan's bones were so tiny and fragile that we probably would've broken his feet. She even had a tough time getting any kind of footprint because (a) she did not want to press too hard and (b) his skin was so fragile that it was starting to peel off. She did give us one ink foot impression print.

It was a draining day for both of us; myself, emotionally, and Tara, both emotionally and physically. Tara had to remain in the hospital for about two hours after the birth, but she wasn't bleeding. Once she had the two hours of Oxytocin, Jules arranged for us to be discharged. We drove home quietly. The sky had clouded over and it looked like rain. Tara talked about feeling a bit cheated with the birth. She hadn't felt empowered as she had after Keena's birth. It wasn't something that I could really comprehend but Tara did discuss this with Jules later. Apparently, many women who use drugs to control the pain feel the same thing. Something in the numbness that the drugs give, also robs those women of some of the positive aspects of the birth.

When we got home, Cailyn was overjoyed to see us. Tara, Cailyn and I lay on our bed talking and snuggled for a bit. We told her what had happened and she said, "I love you, Mommy" and snuggled with Tara. It is hard to know how much little ones comprehend but she seemed to know more than we gave her credit for.

We put Cailyn to bed and then about a half-hour later, we came to bed too. It was very reassuring to have her in bed with us after the events of the day.

As we were falling asleep, a thunder and lightning storm swept by – the only one we've had this summer. The flashes of lightning were brilliant and seemed close yet the thunder was strongly subdued. Maybe it was Faolan saying goodbye.

This was a very sad and trying time but we have to assume that things happen for a reason. We're very sad, of course, but life must go on. We've got Cailyn to remind us of that. But I still can get teary-eyed if I do something like think of the things that Faolan will never see like sunsets or clouds blowing across the sky.

In a few days, we should be getting Faolan's ashes back from the funeral home. We will bury him in the yard and plant a tree for him. Like Keena, he will live in our hearts forever.

"Clare"

If it's not something that you have been through, it is very hard to comprehend the intense feelings of pain, sorrow, emptiness…I could go on. Naively, I used to think it was one of those things that happened to other people or it was more common in some families than others. How wrong can one's perception be.

I have a healthy four year old boy from a previous marriage. There were no complications with him through the pregnancy or labor. I got the dreadful morning sickness for which I had to have a short stay in the hospital on three occasions. My partner has no children and we would love to make our family complete with another couple of kids.

It had taken us seven months to get pregnant. I found out the day I was due to start my period. We were happy as can be. Much to my surprise, I wasn't feeling any sign of sickness at all. I was ecstatic that I wasn't going to feel sick throughout the pregnancy, unlike the last time.

On Friday, I felt achy in my head and just generally, not right. I couldn't put my finger on it, so I rang in sick at work. I was 10 ½ weeks pregnant. It continued through Saturday and brought a very small amount of pink discharge (far from blood). I didn't let this bother me and I told myself it was implantation marks. My partner was working all weekend and on that Sunday, came a little blood. I rang the doctor and got an appointment that day. He took a urine sample. There was more blood than urine. He said I was low in something or other (not sure if it was protein) and booked me in for a scan on Monday morning. My partner got the time off of work to come with me so we sent my son to school and went along to the scan. The lady did the scan and went to get another opinion. They said that I had my dates wrong. I explained that there was no chance of that as it was the first bit of blood. We had also been trying so we knew exactly when the dates were. She said that it was only the sac and that maybe my baby had died four weeks ago. The only way to make sure was to come back a week later and have another scan. I couldn't believe that I had to wait a week to find out if my baby was still alive.

Still dumb-founded, I went to pick up my son from school. My mother-in-law met me and said I looked awfully pale. As we arrived home, I went to the loo, only to find big clots coming away. I was horrified. I frantically fished them out with my marigolds on. I was getting hysterical. I had to take them to the doctor so I would know if it was my baby that had come away. They said I had a choice: they would book me in tomorrow but they would prefer me to have a natural miscarriage. This also horrified me. I went home absolutely torn apart. I tried to continue with the pain and sight of blood clots every time I visited the loo.

Through the evening, the pain progressively got worse and by the early hours, I was passing clots the size of a small piece of liver. We decided that I needed to go to the hospital. We brought my poor son. In hindsight, I wouldn't have done that but I was unaware of the ordeal that I was still to face. The nurse who was doing my drip did it wrong twice and on the third attempt, he got it in. It was the most painful drip I have ever had. We were just left in a cubicle for hours with a bed mat, which was covered in less than a half-hour, as were my hospital and dressing gowns. They finally wheeled me up to the women and children's unit. I got a visit from a couple of nurses. They were horrified at the amount of blood I was losing and they didn't want to do anything until I had another scan which was about six hours away. I was filling one of the paper-mache' bowls every half-hour with clots. By now, the only thing I can say is that it resembled a brain. When I went down for the scan, I got very upset and the nurse looked at me sternly and asked, "Are you in that much pain?" Did this lady know what she just said to me?! I looked at her and said a horrified "no, I am just upset." I could not believe it!

They didn't feed me in case I had to have a D & C. Then come lunchtime, they said I wasn't going to get one so I could have food. They then decided, once I was practically fainting, that they would book me in for the D & C – 17 hours after I had arrived at the hospital. I had the D & C at 8:00 P.M. The doctor said I needed it as I had some tissue stuck in my cervix. I felt so much better after the D & C even though my baby had been removed from me.

I left the hospital the next day after waiting to see the doctor to discharge me. I was anemic yet they didn't have any iron tablets to give me. They said that they had some leaflets with poems but they didn't give them to me. I felt absolutely uneducated in the events that had taken place.

I had two weeks off on sick leave. I don't think I have ever cried so much in my life. After I got home, I looked on the Internet for things relating to miscarriage. I found out that I had actually had what is called a missed miscarriage. It's when your baby dies but stays in your womb and your body continues with the symptoms of pregnancy.

I cannot begin to describe how it felt…heart-wrenching, unimaginable pain, loss, emptiness, despair, guilt and more. These feelings just wash over you in big waves. No one around me really speaks of the loss. My boyfriend hears what I say but he doesn't speak back. You get the definite feeling that people think to themselves, "Oh, is she on about that again?"

I have been obsessive about getting pregnant again to the point where I have lost weight. First, I had to get pregnant the first month after. Then, it was as long as I was pregnant by the time my friend had her baby. Then it had to be before my due date. My partner nags at me for having a cigarette or a glass of wine yet he goes to the pub and gets leathered at least twice a week. He doesn't quite get the "it's as important for him to be healthy as it is me." I know that he wants us to be pregnant again but there is no point in making each other's lives a misery in the process. So we have decided to live life normally and if we get caught, we get caught.

Even now, I have just passed my due date and I have been washed with sorrow again. I took three days' leave from work and made the day special even though my partner ended up going away with work on my due date. The sorrow has come and gone over the last six months and has gotten less consuming and less frequent. I thought once my due date had passed, things would ease off and get back to normal. Today though, I have had this sudden wave of sorrow and sadness and I can't face going back to work. This experience has left me torn. I have always felt like a pretty strong person, yet I have never felt so weak. Some days, I feel depressed and I just can't snap myself out of it.

"Karin"

My name is Karin and I'm 31 years old. I'm married to Mark, who is also 31. We got married on June 2, 2002 in Las Vegas, Nevada after six years of living together. We decided to wait until we got married to try to have a baby so on our wedding night, we decided to let fate take its course. I found out the first of August that I was pregnant.

At six weeks, I started having very light spotting which began on a Saturday afternoon. By Monday, I was panicking. Although the spotting hadn't increased any, it hadn't stopped either. I called the doctor, who had me come in for an HCG test.

The spotting continued so I went back in the next day for another HCG count and ultrasound. They saw a gestational sac but no baby on the ultrasound. My numbers were still increasing from Monday so they asked me to come back in on Thursday to have another blood count.

On Thursday afternoon, my levels had stopped rising and my bleeding had picked up. On Friday, August 23, I had a D & C and my heart broke. I had been seven weeks along.

It took me several weeks to stop crying and get back to some normalcy. The doctor advised Mark and me to wait for at least two cycles to start trying to conceive again. It seemed like an eternity but we did start trying again in November.

We got pregnant again in January and I am happy to report that I am now 34 weeks pregnant and expecting on October 12!

Had it not been for an incredible group of ladies I found in an on-line support group, I most certainly wouldn't have made it through that horrible nightmare, the rigors of trying to conceive again and the scares of going through this pregnancy.

Satchel was born on October 13, 2003. He is the light of my life. Although I often think about the baby we lost, I know that I wouldn't have my little guy with me now if that pregnancy had come to fruition. My husband and I are going to try for number two very soon.

"Kimberly"

I met Ron in the early fall of 2001, just shortly after the tragic events of 9/11. We dated for awhile and pretty much knew right away that it was meant to be. We moved in together in the spring of 2002 and discovered that we were pregnant in April of 2002. I had had severe cramping which led me to call my obstetrician/gynecologist's office. They insisted that I take a pregnancy test before they would schedule me. When it came out positive, they scheduled me for an ultrasound appointment for the next day.

Meanwhile, that evening, the cramping became much worse and Ron took me to the hospital where the doctor told me that I was going to miscarry. He did not do an ultrasound, just a pelvic exam. Being naïve that I was, we went home and waited until the next day.

I kept my appointment with my obstetrician and told him what happened. My obstetrician checked me out and did an ultrasound. We saw a healthy, living fetus. I was six weeks, five days along and I was able to see the heartbeat. We were due on December 28, the same day as her half-sister's birthday. We were so excited. We waited until we were in the second trimester to tell anyone, except close family. I thought we were home-free. I had never known anyone to lose a pregnancy after 12 weeks. The "it can't happen to me" syndrome set in.

My next visits to the doctor went as expected and we had scheduled our mid-pregnancy ultrasound for September 9, 2002. My 20 week appointment went well and the baby was growing normally. We went away for a vacation. When we came back, I felt what I thought were contractions.

At 24 weeks, we headed to the hospital again for a check-up. I was wheeled up to Labor & Delivery and got all dressed in the hospital garments. The nurse came in to hook up the monitors. She couldn't find the heartbeat so she went to find the doctor. My obstetrician came in, wheeling an ultrasound machine and started taking measurements. I thought it was a bit strange that I didn't see any movement so I just waited for the doctor to tell us what was going on. When he finished, he put his hand kindly on my knee and told us that he was sorry but there was no heartbeat and the baby had passed away. We were devastated. All my hopes and dreams were just ripped from my heart. We then had to decide if we wanted to be induced and deliver the baby or if we wanted to let nature take its course and have the baby naturally. We opted for the induction so they scheduled us in for the next day.

Our daughter was born still on September 5, 2002. We named her Kaleigh Ann Caldwell. We were able to hold her that night and the next day. She was so tiny and so fragile. We found out when she was delivered that her umbilical cord had twisted so tightly near her belly-button that it cut off all life supporting supply. A one in a million fluke, we were told. We were instructed to wait three months before trying again. January 2003 came along and we found ourselves pregnant again and due on October 2, 2003. I knew this one would be the one. Our obstetrician wanted to take precautions and wanted plenty of face time with us so we had an ultrasound done right away at seven weeks and scheduled another for 13 weeks. During that ultrasound, the technician noticed an anomaly and went to get the doctor. We were told that the chest wall had not closed and the baby's insides were growing on the outside of its body.

We were sent to a higher level obstetrician out of town for a level two ultrasound. While there, the doctor was none too kind about letting us know that it was not good. Even knowing our past loss, she was very vocal about the outcome being "not so good." I couldn't bear losing another baby. I wasn't going to let it happen. We sat down with the doctor that we had gone to see and he told us that there was no hope for this baby. It had an open chest, organs growing on the outside that were supposed to have gone in around 10 weeks and no diaphragm, meaning the lungs would never develop.

We were faced with another unpreventable loss. I could either carry the baby until it naturally left my body -- even growing until it just stopped living itself or we could have a D & E and remove the fetus. We chose the latter. It was our choice and we felt it was better for the baby to not suffer anymore than it was. Angel Caldwell went to be with her sister on April 11, 2003. Again, a one in a million diagnosis.

I wanted to wait a bit before getting pregnant again. I was terrified of these one in a million hits I was taking. But in August of 2003, we found out we were pregnant again. This time, our obstetrician was very observant and got us in right away for ultrasounds and testing. He even sent us to the level two doctor again for an amniocentesis in December, where, at the last minute, I declined the procedure. I was 29 and fearful that if the results turned out normal and I lost the baby because of the procedure, I would never be able to forgive myself.

We went the rest of the pregnancy event free. At 28 weeks, my obstetrician noticed scar tissue in my uterus and we planned several ultrasounds to make sure it would not get in the baby's way as she grew. She was also breech. At 36 weeks, she was still breech. The doctor did not want to risk turning her as her head was resting on the placenta. He was afraid that the cord might get knotted in the scar tissue so we decided on a C-section at 38 weeks.

On April 19, 2004, our precious daughter, that we had been waiting for, for two years, finally made her presence known in the operating room at 10:33 in the morning.

I think of my two angels everyday and miss them everyday. I know that they live within the child that we were blessed with and see them both in her every time I look at her. I am forever grateful to the staff and technicians at my obstetrician's office and the level two office we were sent to. I am also grateful for the friends that I came to know on the bulletin board at BabyCenter. Without them, I don't know how I would have made it through my losses and my pregnancies.

"Sara"

My name is Sara and my husband's name is Shawn. We have been married for almost seven years now. I got pregnant with my son, who is now six, a month after we got married. When we decided to try again, I never imagined I would miscarry after having had a wonderful pregnancy and delivery with my son.

In July of 2002, I got pregnant. We were thrilled. But a short time after I found out, I just didn't feel pregnant at all. I had no symptoms and at only 10 weeks, I was already showing. I mean, a big belly and I'm a small woman. I just chalked it up to it being nothing.

At 12 weeks along, I started spotting. I still figured things were okay and thought I was just overdoing it. As the night wore on, I was spotting more and more. I went to the emergency room and unfortunately, I had to wait almost three hours. I decided to just go home and wait until morning and go to my regular doctor.

That morning, I was still spotting so I went on in with my mother-in-law because my husband had to work. My doctor did an exam and afterwards, I could tell by his face that something was wrong. He didn't say anything yet…he wanted me to have an ultrasound first. I had to wait almost two hours and it was awful waiting!

When I finally had the ultrasound, the technician said right away she couldn't find a heartbeat. I was only measuring eight weeks. I just burst out crying. My husband came to the hospital right away and he cried all the way there. I had to have a D & C later on that night because I was bleeding so much. The worst part was being on the same floor as the newborns.

It took a long while to get over it but I decided I was determined to have a healthy baby. Three months afterwards, we started trying again. It didn't take long and I was pregnant. The first 12 weeks were nerve-wracking…but after that, it flew by. We now have a very healthy baby girl named Lauren Noelle and she is full of energy!

I think about my baby in heaven all the time and I can't wait to get to meet him or her one day.

"Gwen"

We had waited almost two hours in the waiting room. During that time, I found myself thinking back to my appointment nearly three weeks before. I had seen my precious baby on the ultrasound screen. She was just starting to look like a baby. At eight weeks' gestation, you could just barely see a flicker of a heartbeat. She measured almost two weeks smaller than she should have.

My doctor kept looking at the screen. I said, "Is everything okay? He assured me it was. But I could tell he was keeping something from me. I felt uneasy when he asked me to come back in two weeks for another ultrasound.

Since that time, I had worried over not having any pregnancy symptoms. My first pregnancy brought with it food aversion, vomiting and migraine headaches. This time, I felt nothing. A voice whispered in my heart, "You will never hold this baby in your arms." But I kept ignoring it, believing that nothing like that would ever happen to me.

"Grubb," the nurse called. My three year old daughter, my husband and I walked back the long hall to the examining room. We had brought my daughter with us to see the baby that she had begun to call "Ellie." She was sure she would be getting a sister. When the doctor came in, he apologized for keeping us waiting. He had been in emergency surgery for an ectopic pregnancy. I think I said something like, "Oh, how sad!" I think back to the irony of my words that day.

He put the Doppler on my belly and the ultrasound picture came up on the screen. I could tell right away something was horribly wrong. I was almost 11 weeks pregnant but there wasn't anything in my uterus that resembled a baby. The doctor touched my arm and said, "I'm sorry, honey." He didn't even need to explain. I knew my baby was dead. I began to cry. Everything after that is pretty much a blur. I had blood work done to confirm what the ultrasound showed. A D & C was scheduled for two days later.

Despite my doctor's assurance that there was nothing I could have done to prevent the miscarriage, I went over and over in my mind what could have caused it. I didn't care that he said it was just a chromosomal abnormality. Was it something I ate, a medicine I took, some activity I did? Surely I could have prevented it. A part of me had died. All my dreams and hopes wiped away. There was no consoling me.

No one understood how I felt, not even my husband. Then I found a group of ladies on-line who were going through the same thing as me. I think it was about a week after my D & C that I came across the support group on Babycenter.com. It was for women who had miscarriages that August or September. If I had not had the support of those women, I don't know how I would have made it through the sleepless nights and the long days that followed. When everyone around me, including my husband, couldn't understand why I was still mourning, they did. When no one else remembered that it was my baby's due date, they did. And when I got pregnant again and everyone else thought it should take away the pain of the miscarriage, they knew it didn't. We now have our own private group on-line. We have never met in person, but they are like sisters to me. I thank God He sent them to me in my time of need.

I became pregnant again right away, about two weeks after my D & C. I was scared to death of another miscarriage. This pregnancy came and went without a single problem. I now have a very healthy, active two year old boy. And God gave me another surprise. I also have a very healthy baby boy! I certainly have my hands full but I wouldn't change a thing for the world.

I believe our "Ellie" didn't live and die in vain. Her short life gave me an invaluable lesson. I learned to not take anything for granted.

We can say that life is a miracle, but I never fully comprehended what a gift it is until it was taken from me. I know Ellie is watching over us. She is my children's guardian angel. And when we meet in heaven someday, I will finally get to hold her in my arms and tell her how much I love her.

"Hannah"

It's Friday, February 7, and I am seven and a half weeks pregnant with my third child. It's actually my fourth pregnancy as I miscarried the first time I was pregnant. I have two beautiful, healthy children who are now 22 months and 7 months old. If someone would have asked me five years ago if I had planned on having my children so close in age, I would have said, "No way!" In fact, I had always wanted to space two or three years in between each child. Unfortunately, I have learned that things do not always turn out the way you want.

I was so happy when I got pregnant on the first try and we looked forward to welcoming our third child. My due date was set for September 29, the day before my 29th birthday. What a great birthday present, I thought from the moment I "passed" the home pregnancy test.

So today is the day of my first pre-natal appointment and as with all of my other pregnancies, G. has insisted on accompanying me. Being that we're going to see our baby's heartbeat on an ultrasound today, he says that he wouldn't miss it for the world. I wouldn't even think of refusing him, especially because I am nervous about this appointment. Having gone through a miscarriage, I don't think that I will ever walk into an obstetrician's office without the slightest bit of anxiety. I could probably go on to have ten kids and I will still feel nervous about waiting those few minutes to hear or see a baby's heartbeat. I didn't feel that way the first time I was pregnant. Then again, I didn't expect to miscarry. I had been so ignorant, thinking that nothing bad would ever happen to me. When I did miscarry, it changed me forever. It made me realize that you cannot take anything for granted. I will never again feel that secure, going into that appointment to see my baby for the first time on an ultrasound screen.

The nurse weighs me, tests my urine for protein and sugar, and takes my blood pressure. So far, everything checks out fine. We're taken into an examination room where I am told to get undressed and wait for the doctor. With this being my fourth pregnancy in less than three years, I am pretty familiar with the protocol.

My obstetrician arrives and congratulates us on the pregnancy. Noting that I was at his office a mere five months ago for a post-partum check-up, he jokes that I should get a frequent visitor card. With G. by my side, the doctor examines me and confirms that I am most definitely pregnant. He then turns on his ultrasound equipment and tells me that we're going to see what is going on inside.

G. holds my hand as I wait for the doctor to show us the heartbeat. It seems like hours go by before the doctor asks us if we're sure about the time I conceived. We tell him that yes, we are positive. The doctor then gently tells us that the fetus stopped developing at five weeks…there is no growth. When I ask him if seven and a half weeks is too early in the pregnancy to detect a heartbeat, he says it's not. He would have been able to see a heartbeat even a few days ago, he says. He calls this a blighted ovum, which means that a fertilized egg has died. G. and I are both speechless as the doctor admits that he is pretty sure that this pregnancy isn't going to work out but that there is the slightest chance that he could be wrong. He tells us that we will know for sure within the next week.

Having been through this before, we know better than to doubt a medical professional's word. We look sadly at each other and then back to the doctor. He instructs me to go home and wait out the next few days. He explains that I will probably start bleeding in the next few days but that if I don't miscarry on my own by Tuesday, I will have to have a D & C. He also suggests that I see a radiologist next Wednesday for an ultrasound to confirm his diagnosis. In any case, he wants me to keep him informed of what is happening. Before he leaves us to take in what has happened in the last few minutes, he gives me a hug and tells us both that he is very sorry. He confides that his wife had a miscarriage and that he knows what we are going through.

G. and I go home together in total disbelief. He decides to stay home with me and the kids, rather than go to work. As he sits down on the couch to play with the kids, I go to tell our Au Pair about our appointment. She cries when I tell her that I am probably going to miscarry. I try to be stoic but inside, I am hurting. I cannot believe that I am going to lose yet another baby!

As I watch my daughter playing with her baby brother, I realize how truly lucky I am to have them. Yes, I am sad that we're not going to have another baby right now but I do have two wonderful children who are alive and healthy. If I would never be able to have another baby, I would still have them. That, in itself, makes this miscarriage easier to handle than my first miscarriage, when I didn't have any children toddling around the house. Of course, I would never refer to any miscarriage as "easy."

I call the radiologist's office and make an appointment for 8:00 A.M. on Wednesday. When the receptionist questions the purpose of my visit, I calmly tell her that I need to confirm a diagnosis of a threatened early miscarriage. After she says she is sorry and she gives me the instructions for the ultrasound, she suggests I call her if I need to cancel my appointment. I respond that I would love to have to cancel this appointment and then I hang up.

This wasn't supposed to happen a second time, dammit! I thought my first miscarriage was a freak thing and that it wouldn't happen again. That is what my previous doctor had told me at the time. Had she been lying? Or is just a matter of her not having known that I am obviously susceptible to first term miscarriage.

I start to ask myself all kinds of questions. Is there something wrong with me, that this is the second time I've had an unsuccessful pregnancy? What did I do wrong this time? Did I take this all for granted? Do I have to go through a miscarriage every time I deliver a healthy baby?

Every time I go to the bathroom over the next few days, I look to see if I'm bleeding. I'm not. I don't know whether to feel relieved or whether I should assume that it's just a matter of time before I miscarry. I can't imagine that the doctor would prepare me for a miscarriage if I wasn't going to have one. He did tell us that there was a slim possibility that he could be wrong but he also told us that he hasn't been wrong about this before.

The doctor calls on Monday morning to see how I'm doing. I report to him that I haven't started to bleed yet or feel any cramping. He tells me to let him know if anything happens in the next 48 hours; otherwise, we will talk after I have the ultrasound on Wednesday. I confide to him that I hate having to wait this out. I recall how, when I had my first miscarriage, I had a D & C performed within hours after learning the fetus wasn't viable. In retrospect, I walked around for weeks with a dead fetus inside of me but I didn't know that anything was wrong at the time. In this case, it's only a matter of days but I am "in the know." I don't know which scenario is worse. The doctor says it's important that we give this a few more days; we'll know once and for all when we go for the ultrasound. Before he hangs up, he reminds me that he's there for us, day or night.

My doctor's office calls shortly thereafter and tells me that they have made arrangements for my D & C. I am instructed to have some blood work done today as part of the pre-registration process and then return on Thursday for the D & C at 7:00 A.M.

With my ultrasound set for tomorrow morning and the blood work done, I am ready to say goodbye to this pregnancy. Of course, I am still hopeful that the doctor is wrong...that I will never start to bleed because there isn't going to be a miscarriage. But I know deep down that he isn't wrong. I just want this miscarriage to be over and done with already. Knowing that I am all set for the D & C, I don't want to have to go through a miscarriage at home. I want to be put to sleep for 45 minutes and wake up, knowing that the nightmare is finally over for us and that we can get on with our lives.

G. clears his calendar for Thursday so that he can be with me for the D & C and then afterwards, at home. As I put the kids to sleep that night, I thank God that I have my two sweet, beautiful children who are totally oblivious to what their parents are going through. We have been so careful about what we have said and done in front of them over these past several days and of course, they don't even know I'm pregnant. I guess that old saying is right...what they don't know won't hurt them.

It's hard though, not being able to share my pain with any of my friends and extended family. Even if I weren't facing a miscarriage, it would be too early for us to share our expectant news with everyone. Keeping good news to yourself is hard but you know that you will be making an announcement eventually. Keeping sad news like a miscarriage is doubly hard because you are in pain and you want to share it with those you love. I know that until I actually see my baby on an ultrasound and know that it has no future, I cannot share my pain with anyone. It's not as if I can call up a friend right now and say, "How are you? I'm having an ultrasound done tomorrow to see if my baby is dead or alive!"

Thank goodness for G., though. He is my rock and so much more. I know he's hurting just as much as I am but all he cares about is me. He is constantly asking me what I'm thinking about, how I'm feeling, if I need anything. When I ask him the same questions, he replies he's fine. He says that the loss is easier this time since we already have kids. We're also prepared this time, which makes a big difference.

Before I go to sleep for the night, I pray to God that the radiologist will prove my doctor wrong tomorrow. I know I am asking the impossible but I can still ask, can't I?!

I don't sleep well at all. I'm constantly tossing and turning, thinking about what will happen tomorrow. I start to feel cramps during the night but I try not to think about it. It's probably something I ate at dinner that didn't agree with me. At 4:00 A.M., I go to the bathroom for probably my fifth time that night. Something tells me to put the light on in the bathroom. I am hardly prepared when I discover blood in the toilet. And when I wipe myself, I find a red clot of blood on the toilet paper. My eyes are hardly open but I know that this clot is my baby. I suddenly feel very dirty and impure and violated. It's exactly the way I used to feel every time I got a period when I was trying to get pregnant.

Not thinking clearly, I throw the toilet paper into the toilet and flush it. I probably should have saved it for lab work or whatever they do on dead fetuses but at this moment, I can't worry about such things. I sit on the toilet, rocking back and forth and ask God why He let this happen to us again. And why did He make me go through seeing my baby leave my body? Is this the memory I get to keep of my fourth pregnancy?! I don't feel angry at Him like I did the first time I miscarried and I don't lack any faith in Him. I just don't understand why this happened a first, and now, a second time.

I return to bed and tell a groggy G. that I lost the baby. He says something about the nightmare finally being over but I tell him that I'd much rather have slept through the loss via a D & C. He goes back to sleep but I remain awake for the rest of the night/morning, recalling vivid images of the bloody fetus.

I call the radiologist's office at 7:30 to inform them that I had the miscarriage and I won't be having the ultrasound after all. I call the doctor's office at 9:15 and leave a message that I need to speak to him at once. He returns my call within the hour and offers me comforting words upon hearing of my miscarriage. He says it's much better to go through it at home rather than go through the grueling D & C procedure. When I mentioned that I flushed the bloody remains down the toilet without thinking about it, he says there was nothing we could have found out from any lab work. After he tells me that he will cancel the D & C for me, he says I can try to get pregnant again whenever I'm ready. I'm surprised to hear this, considering that I had to wait three months the last time I miscarried. My doctor reminds me that I didn't go through a D & C this time so my body is ready whenever I am.

Although I am hardly in the mood to start trying for another pregnancy right now, I know that I will be emotionally ready in a few weeks. I tell my doctor before I hang up that I hope to see him soon.

"Alan"

Sara and I have gone through two second-trimester miscarriages. Both of them took place at virtually the same point - about 18 weeks into the pregnancy - approximately five and a half years apart.

When we experienced the first of these miscarriages, my feelings were mainly about Sara and how she would cope. I remember taking her phone call from the obstetrician's office and sensing instantly how overwhelming the loss was and would be for her.

The period leading up to the pregnancy had been stressful and I hadn't been sure that I was ready for another baby. In fact, Sara was convinced that I did not want the pregnancy at all. Given all of this, I felt partially responsible when the miscarriage happened.

For me, the loss of this pregnancy was just that – it had been 'only' a pregnancy. As a father, the pregnancy had not yet become for me a life, a baby. It remained abstract, an idea. Sara told me repeatedly that for her, it was obviously different: she had the baby inside her and she could feel it developing. I understood this but I think she still felt that I couldn't understand what she was going through.

In the months afterwards, I spent my energy on helping Sara cope and trying to keep some sense of normalcy in our household. I didn't spend any energy on thinking about my own feelings except for my sense of guilt.

The second miscarriage was much more intense and difficult for me. We had tried for about a year to get pregnant which was, in itself, a painful experience. I felt helpless watching Sara agonize every month to see if she was pregnant or not and trying to overcome her deep disappointment each time. When we finally succeeded and the pregnancy progressed for a few weeks, I was relieved and happy. I knew from our past experience that something could happen but I really didn't expect it. I thought we had paid our dues, so to speak. When Sara called to say "We lost this one too," I was shocked.

Five years of thinking had taught us much about how we'd dealt with the first miscarriage. This was reflected especially in how we handled the actual physical removal of the baby each time. With the first loss, Sara underwent a D & E. She wasn't fully awake for the procedure and I wasn't in the room when it was performed. When it was over, there was no fetus and that was it. We realized with hindsight that this had been a mistake. It did not allow us the mourning that we needed, though at the time, we weren't even aware of that.

This time, the obstetrician felt that she should actually deliver the baby. At first, this sounded cruel. Why be forced to go through that for nothing? Sara said she wanted it this way, as at least the baby would emerge intact and she would be able to see it. I was with her throughout this process. When the baby was delivered, a nurse photographed him so we could at least have something tangible, a visual memory. And, because Jewish law requires the burial of a fetus that is delivered naturally, we had to make arrangements with a funeral home. We had to talk about burial, cemeteries, a marker and most poignant of all, giving the baby a name. All of this made me feel very much that we had lost a human life, not 'just' a pregnancy. And it was a life we had never gotten to know.

I still feel cheated about this loss, particularly since we don't know if we will be able to try again to become pregnant. I don't try to understand it or find meaning in it – I don't think this is possible. As a religious person, I wonder if there is anything we could have done differently in a metaphysical sense to allow us to have the baby that we had wanted.

We had kept our first miscarriage a private matter and attempted to deal with it on our own. We were relatively new in our community and we didn't know how to reach out to others for help of any type. The second time, we told a few people what had happened and we were almost instantly flooded with support in the form of phone calls, letters, food and much more. The conventional wisdom is that men do their grieving alone but for me, the opportunity to talk to others during the weeks following the loss was crucial. Many people came to me and said things like, "I know there's nothing that I can say except that we are thinking of you." These sentiments are what helped carry me through.

"Jane"

I had my third miscarriage 18 months after giving birth to my son. Due to an understaffed hospital, a common problem of disproportion turned into an obstetric emergency. I was told that both the baby and I could die. I was then left for two hours (fully dilated) while I waited to go to theatre. My son was delivered by forceps in a fairly violent manner which involved me pushing myself down the bed while semi-paralyzed. His shoulders got stuck and I had an extensive episiotomy. He required resuscitation and treatment in Special Care with intravenous antibiotics. I was unable to breastfeed and I felt terrible guilty about it. My son was very fortunate to have no other birth injuries apart from a forceps scar next to his eye and a bruised area on his face.

Six months after giving birth, my husband's rheumatologist wanted to put my husband on Methotrexate. You cannot try for a baby while on this drug and for six months afterwards. When my son was 18 months old, my husband's arthritis necessitated the drug. We arranged to have semen stored. In the last month before he started the drug, I got pregnant. This is the diary of trying to come to terms with a third miscarriage and possible infertility while raising a toddler and coming to terms with a very traumatic birth experience.

One week after:

"There is no heartbeat, is there?"

"No, I am afraid I can't see one."

Eight weeks and three days. Eight weeks was supposedly a viable pregnancy. I had my scan with a heartbeat and got a picture to show everyone. Maybe it died three days later or maybe it clung on for another week and just stopped growing. Either way, it was floating around. A fetus still in the dark waters. Still, but my body didn't know. Only a slight warning sign of a small bit of blood but no more. My body showed no signs of giving up on the silent traveler. As the nurse said, "I obviously have a problem letting go."

I was so controlled. I asked all the questions I wish I had asked after the second miscarriage. I looked and looked at the screen and I didn't cry. I started to collapse into tears behind the curtain when I was getting dressed. I couldn't get my legs into my pants. But then, I had to gulp down the tears because I didn't want to scare Connor.

My Connor, my angel…I was so lucky to have him and I knew that. It was that knowledge and pure shock that allowed me to remain controlled for a good week afterwards. As long as it took to put on a face to meet all the faces that I meet. To make sure that everyone else is not too disappointed. That everyone else knows that there is nothing that they could have done. To make sure that no one escapes me. I had learned from the times before, not to allow anyone not to speak to me. Not to allow them to run away and avoid the difficult situation. So one by one, I met them all.

We all revel in our normality. Normal talk about everyone's normal world. I am proud of my bravery. I am pleased that I have made everyone face me. There is little or no talk of the silent traveler. The extinguished light that was painlessly, cleanly taken from me. Taken away so clinically because my body was failing to comprehend what it had lost. I had wanted the pain, the mess, the crying, and the labor. To truly know and see what I had lost. Instead, I concentrate on getting through the anesthetic. How brave I am to go into theatre again. How quickly I can walk around afterwards. Return to normal. Allow everyone to be as normal. But after a while, the body must inevitably notice. Hormones begin to crash right at the point when no mention is made of

the silent traveler. No "how are you?" I am brave but going to see a pregnant woman who is only a few weeks ahead of me, is beyond me today. I am ashamed of this but there is a crack in my armor. I am too jealous. Maybe if she knew but my friend, who is her friend, has not told her even though I said she could. To pretend that I was ill last week
is more than I can bear when my body is screaming out for my baby!
My baby! My baby!

All of a sudden, at the most inconvenient time, my body knows. It knows it has lost and it mourns. Not the quiet, tearful mourning of last week but an angry but silent howl that wells up inside. It longs to be released but normality hems it back in until a black cloak of sadness and self-disgust envelops me. I am unable to feed myself properly. I don't seem to remember how. I have no time off. It is not just about me. I could mourn but I need to be with Connor. I want to be with Connor but everywhere we go is too normal. My time-scale is behind everyone else's. Other people are forgetting at the time that my shock has faded into a stark remembrance of exactly what I have lost.

Two months after:

I am having my second period today. My pregnancy would have been 18 weeks along. I got the most insensitive text message from L and K's 10 week healthy fetus and about not telling C yet. It was like being stabbed in the heart. But I have cried for a bit now and I am back to being numb. I hate being numb and I hate it that people think I am so hard. How on earth could L not see how that would make me feel? I want to be out of her circle of friends. She is being voyeuristic about my grief. She won't be satisfied until she sees my face when I see the babies. It seems it is fun to watch to see how far I can go. To see if I will ever crack. I can't tolerate it. I am jealous. I miss my baby.

I have to come to terms with the possibility of never having another. They are not helping. They make me feel desperate…that I must have another. It doesn't help because there won't necessarily be another and not on their time-scale. And it wouldn't be a normal experience.

Two and a half months after – Christmas holiday:

64

I felt terrible when we came back from Ireland. A mixture of shock at the tsunami, Christmas-anti climax and jet lag resulted in me being able to tap into my grief for my lost baby. I really sobbed, howled and felt shock like I was still in the scan room. I put my hands over my face and took up back where I had left off when I realized in the scan room that I had to stop crying for Connor's sake. I got the sleep-suit I had bought for the baby out of the wardrobe. I was nearly knocked over by the grief.

It was long overdue. I have felt better since partly because I realize how much I did love it and it was very much wanted. I realized that I can purely feel grief for my baby. I can't believe quite how much has been suppressed.

Today:

It is very close to the baby's due date. After my previous two miscarriages, I had been pregnant or trying by now. This is so different. I had a mock insemination but that was as far as I got. My husband is off his Methotrexate and it remains to be seen if he can stay off it for six months. If he can, we can try again normally. I am going to the GP tomorrow to ask for repeat blood clotting tests. I can't believe the consultant could say that a blood clotting problem is the most likely cause but then say he is not going to re-test me or put me on aspirin again. I hope the GP will help. I need to know what I am up against before I can try again. I also need another ultrasound so they can properly look at my womb.

Connor is getting bigger and more independent by the day. I have time now with my arms free of a child. In some ways, this makes me miss my baby terribly but it is also good for me in that I am having to be myself again. This helps me to see how life can still be great if we are to be a one child family. Who knows what the future holds? I try my best to leave it in God's hands.

"Darlanne"

Tuesday, September 23, 2003 was quite possibly the happiest day of our lives. After years of trying and months of heartbreak, two of the most beautiful lines brought a joy to our hearts that we had never felt before. We were going to have a baby! Oh my goodness, how my heart filled so completely full of pride and love.

I actually had a feeling that I might be pregnant but after trying for so long, I had basically dismissed that what I was feeling, was more psychological than anything else, much less the possibility of truly being pregnant. I just thought it was never going to happen without the assistance of a fertility specialist. After all, last we heard, IVF/ICSI would be our only option. Well, we were preparing ourselves for that and then a miracle happened. I swear that is exactly what it was, a blessed miracle.

For a couple of days after finding out that we were going to become parents, we just kept it to ourselves. Our little secret. It felt so good to be happy about something so incredibly beautiful. But after a few days, I couldn't take it any longer. I had to tell someone. On my way out to run an errand for work, I got my phone from out of my purse and called my friend, Tammy. "Guess what?" is how I started off the conversation. I am sure she thought I had some juicy gossip but it wasn't what she thought. Being able to say the words out loud to someone other than Jim felt so confirming. As tears of joy streamed down my face, I finally got the words out, "I am pregnant." Tammy immediately started crying…she was so happy for us. She knew our struggle and how much this meant to us. It felt so good to tell someone.

Later, I told Jim that I had told Tammy so it was only fair that he got to tell someone. Later that evening, my wonderful sister-in-law stopped by the house. When she walked in, I handed her the baggie that contained the positive pregnancy test stick. "What do you think this means?" I asked her. Suddenly, a deafening scream filled the house. As she jumped up and down screaming, I stood there taking it all in. Finally, it was our turn and it felt wonderful! We kept quiet again for a couple of more days, enjoying our secret and contemplated who we would tell next.

That weekend, we visited our families and shared the news. Everyone was as happy as we were. Well, maybe not as happy but close. The days that followed were nothing less than pure joy, even the morning sickness. I adored every last second of it!

October 20, 2003 was my first visit to the obstetrician. It was glorious! I was so excited yet cautious. Up to this point in my life, I had been pregnant three times and I had no living children, needless to say. As happy as I was, I was still very scared. My doctor was more than I could have ever asked for. She said everything looked perfect but due to my history, she felt I deserved to know that everything was okay. So the following day, on my mother-in-law's birthday, she scheduled an ultrasound. Anticipating my first glimpse at the precious baby growing inside of me, I could barely sleep a wink. The excitement was incredible. It was the longest 14 hours of my life.

Finally, at 1:00 P.M., on October 21, my husband and I were patiently waiting to hear my name called to go back and prepare to see our child on the ultrasound. Finally, the door opened and we were asked to go back to the ultrasound room.

As I lay there waiting for my doctor to join us, my emotions were crazy. I refused to let any negative thoughts enter my mind. This was going to be wonderful. We were going to see a heartbeat. We were going to see our baby.

The doctor came in smiling, ready to share the incredible news that was waiting for us on the other side of the ultrasound wand. All of a sudden, I heard that beautiful swishing sound of a baby's heartbeat. I looked at the screen and there was our baby. Our miracle, we both cried. It was the most beautiful day of our lives. My heart felt so much relief. She confirmed that I was nine weeks along and things looked awesome! I am pretty sure winning the lottery could not have made us any happier than we were at that moment in time.

My pregnancy was progressing beautifully. My clothes began to get uncomfortable. I was loving it! Never in my life, had I been so excited about getting bigger. But because of my history, I was hesitant to rush out and buy maternity clothes. It was becoming necessary so I bit the bullet and the Saturday after Thanksgiving, my husband and I bought my first maternity outfit.

The next day, even though our baby was "hiding," we had what I consider to be our first official family photo, complete with our loyal Lab, Libby. Our family! God, I loved how that sounded.

The first days in December of 2003, I had been experiencing some pressure in my lower abdomen but since I was three weeks past the 12 week mark, that mythical "safe" point, I didn't think anything about it. All natural, I thought. The baby is growing, my uterus is making room for my sweet baby and this is what happens during pregnancy…no big deal.

On December 4, I went to work. The day was uneventful but that evening, I was so exhausted that I was in bed by 7:00 P.M.

On Friday, December 5, the alarm went off. It was time to get ready for work. I went into the bathroom, ran myself a lukewarm bath and gently slid into the tub. Something didn't feel quite right but I couldn't put my finger on it. I went to work and about mid-morning, I noticed the pressure was becoming a little more uncomfortable. I still thought this went with the territory. To ease my mind, I called my sister-in-law and she said she had felt the same way and not to really worry.

I kept repeating to myself what the doctor had said the last time I went in for an ultrasound. "Your risk of miscarriage is now at less than 5%." I refused to believe anything was going to happen to this baby, even though deep down, I knew something was wrong. I worked with my mother-in-law and I told her how I was feeling and she agreed that it sounded normal. But at the end of the day, the pressure was much worse and I called my doctor's office. They told me that it sounded like I could possibly be miscarrying but there was nothing that they could really do. They advised me to go home, put my feet up and rest.

"This pregnancy cannot end. We were going to look at baby furniture tonight!" I thought to myself. My mother-in-law knew I was worried. She begged me to let her follow me home but I told her that everything was going to be fine and I just needed to lay down.

As I drove home, the pain was nauseating. I couldn't believe how intense the pain was. It was then that I knew something very bad was wrong. I made it to my house and struggled to get to the couch. I went into the bathroom because I felt like I was going to throw up. I was so uncomfortable. I started taking my clothes off as fast as I could and without any warning, I heard my water break. Tears just started to stream down my face and the only thought that ran through my mind was, "No! I am dreaming this. I know I am. No, God, no." Pleading and begging for it all to stop.

My poor dog was outside the bathroom door, whimpering uncontrollably. Without realizing it, I had begun to push and within seconds, I had James' little body in my hands. I was trembling terribly and there was blood everywhere but I just stood there, crying and holding my baby.

I somehow managed to find a container to place his body in since I knew they would do testing on him, and the entire time, I felt like I was watching someone else go through this. It was so surreal. I wanted my husband there so bad. The house had never felt so empty or scary. Still in pain, I called my precious husband at work. All I could do was cry. When I talked to him earlier in the day, we had made plans to go look at baby furniture that evening. Now, I was calling him to tell him our baby had died. After calling him and sharing our horrible news, I called the doctor's office and was advised to go to the hospital.

My sweet dog was frantic…she had no idea what was going on but she could tell something was terrible wrong. She would not leave my side. I had to dress myself two times because I was bleeding.

When Jim got home, I was sitting in the kitchen holding James. All we could do was cry. We got to the hospital and suddenly, I became numb. I had tears streaming down my face but I felt nothing. My sweet doctor comforted us and told us that it sounded like an incompetent cervix. She reassured us that she would get us a baby.

Two days later, the dark sadness, pain and emptiness hit me like a ton of bricks. It was literally a living hell. I thought my arms would never stop aching. It was so agonizing. Now, I realize I have survived something that at first, I didn't think I ever would. My marriage has only gotten stronger. I am now able to see the other side of sadness. I am now able to feel happiness. But my James still does and always will be my greatest heartbreak and my greatest love.

"Hannah"

It's Friday, March 26, 1999. My period isn't due for another two days but something besides a very anxious husband is telling me to go ahead and do a home pregnancy test. I've been feeling nauseous for the past two or three days but I keep telling myself that it's too soon for morning sickness. And besides, I never felt queasy until a few weeks into my other pregnancies.

I have kept a box of Fact Plus hidden in my bathroom closet since I was last pregnant in 1997. G. stands by my side while we nervously await the test results. We definitely see a negative line but we think we see a faint vertical line as well. It's too hard to tell!

We take turns holding up the test to the light to make sure that we really see what looks like a plus sign. Since we're not sure if our eyes are playing tricks on us, we decide to wait until Sunday to do another pregnancy test.

On Sunday, I do a second test and once again, I see what I think is a faint vertical line a few minutes after the red color appears in the window. I wonder aloud if I read the results too late. The test instruction mentions that you must read the result right away and that if you wait too long, the chemicals in the test might cause a false positive sign to appear. I swear that I'm hallucinating but I do see what looks like a positive sign. And I am officially late with my period. Okay, okay…it's only an hour late but I am so regular with my cycle that I can know that I'm pregnant if I don't get my period by a certain time of the day. And that certain time of the day has passed! As nervous as I am about having four kids under five, I am excited. On Monday, I do yet another test and once again, it's faintly positive. I wonder aloud to G. that my HCG levels might be low and that is why there isn't a stronger positive sign.

Since we're leaving on Tuesday to go out of town, we agree to wait until Wednesday to share our good news with his parents in person. I do phone my obstetrician's office though and make my first pre-natal appointment for April 26.

We're in Florida now. I stay behind in our hotel room to watch the kids while G. goes off to tell his parents. He returns 15 minutes later and assures me that his mom and dad are thrilled with the news. That night, his parents congratulate me and tell me that they are looking forward to our December baby.

On Thursday afternoon, I get up to go to the bathroom while G. and the kids are all napping. I am horrified when I notice blood on the tissue. I yell out for G. to come to the bathroom right away. He runs into the bathroom and I tell him I saw blood on the tissue. I try to assure myself that I'm just spotting, something that I have never experienced in my previous pregnancies. But being the type A person that I am, I decide to call my obstetrician's office and report the blood. With my doctor being off for the day, a nurse takes my call and asks if I'm experiencing any back pain, cramping or clotting. I tell her no. I don't feel any different than I have felt the past few days. She instructs me to stay in bed until the next morning but to call immediately if anything else happens. And if everything remains status quo during the night, I should call the office tomorrow at 9:00.

I fill G. in on the call and get into bed. During the next hour, I get up several times to go to the bathroom and I start to see more blood on the tissue even though G. orders me not to look. At one point, I notice a few drops of blood coming out with my urine. I burst into tears and tell G. that this isn't just spotting. I know that I am having a miscarriage. I try to remain calm, as not to let on to the kids that something is wrong. G. asks me if I'm okay. I tell him with tears in my eyes that I am sad but that I had a feeling that something wasn't right from the beginning. I ask him if he's okay. He responds that he's sad too but that this is happening to me right now more than it is to us. When I go to the bathroom an hour and a half after that first "spotting" episode, I see a small clot in the toilet and I get this terrible, sinking feeling. I'm losing yet another pregnancy!

When I had my first miscarriage five years ago, I was told that it most likely wouldn't happen again. Then, I miscarried two years ago. But with each miscarriage, I went on to have healthy babies.

I decide to join my family for dinner that night. I start to feel cramps so I go to the bathroom. I feel the same dirty and violated feeling that I had had two other times, as I see the first of many heavy clots to come out of me. I look at what was supposed to be my baby in the toilet and say a sad goodbye to him/her.

During dinner, I try not to let on to anyone at the table that anything is wrong. G. has shared the bad news with his parents but neither of them says anything. It's amazing that just 24 hours ago, they were wishing us well with the pregnancy.

I call my obstetrician's office the next morning and report the miscarriage to my doctor. I ask him if I have to take any precautions for a subsequent pregnancy since I've now suffered three miscarriages. He responds no…that this kind of miscarriage, an early miscarriage or a "missed period," happens more often than not.

I try to remain philosophical about this miscarriage. It was very early and we weren't as invested in it as we were with the other ones. We are still sad though. This was a baby we wanted and planned to have. I guess there is another plan in store for us. When we are truly ready for baby number four, it will come and everything will be just right.

"Jenna"

***The names in this story have been initialed for privacy reasons.

I am ashamed to admit it but we were not thrilled when I found out I was expecting our fourth child. We had established a rhythm, an outlook on our future that didn't include a fourth. Some days, I cried in fear. But we knew that as the months went by, we would adjust and we did.

No one seemed more excited than our three older children. They talked to their little sibling and sang to him, often pulling up my shirt in public to do so. As he grew bigger and I started feeling its movements, I grew more and more excited at all the things we would do with our baby. I bought clothes, diapers, a sling…and dreamed of nursing this new baby and taking long walks with him. Our last…the fulfillment of our family and our love.

On a Monday in late February, when I was eight months pregnant, I went to see my midwife, T. The heartbeat was strong, the baby active. We joked about the rowdy babies I made and T. told me how lucky I was to be having my fourth healthy child.

It was Saturday afternoon when I first became concerned that I had not felt the baby move in some time. By 9:00, after I had had a big glass of juice and a bath, I was sure something was wrong. I woke my husband and we discussed it. He reminded me that I had panicked in all my earlier pregnancies, going to the midwife, and everything had been fine. He was right. I went to sleep.

By the next morning, I still had felt nothing. I called T. and she told us to come right over. B. tried to get me to eat lunch but I couldn't. He shook his head and said, "I'm sure you've got yourself all worked up. You'll be hungry after we see T."

We went to her house, saying little on the long drive. Her first question to me was, "Do you feel pregnant?" I just shook my head at her and said nothing.

We got the kids to play in the den and went to the exam room. She turned on the ultrasound. There was no heartbeat. There was nothing on the Doppler. She didn't have to say anything. She simply started crying.

T. went to make some phone calls. B. called the kids in. He was direct. "We have bad news. T. can't find a heartbeat. It looks like our baby has died."

M. responded with the question that would come to haunt us… "Why?"

We got ready to go. I called a friend in my church, who would call the pastors and prayer chain. B. called our neighbor, C., to be with the kids.

When we got home, C. and her son were waiting. I got out and she put her arms around me. I sobbed, "The baby died." She held me there in front of our house while I cried. We dropped the kids off, picked up our digital camera and headed for the hospital. How to describe the experience? Aside from getting admitted, there was paperwork and questions to be answered. Did we want a lock of hair, pictures, a hat and gown? So many things to decide at once. One of the pastors came to call and prayed with us.

I was taken for a brief ultrasound. The technician and a doctor confirmed that there was no heartbeat. The small shred of hope I had been clinging to, died. The doctor on call asked if I wanted to be induced now or wait until the next day. I decided it would be best to have this part over with so Pitocin was started. I had decided that while I had had three natural births, there was no reason to do that this time. After all, why do we avoid drugs in labor?

Our newest pastor came to visit. It turns out that this was her first pastoral care call. She was so wonderful. She stayed over an hour listening to us, praying with us and reading the Scriptures.

After she left, I dozed on and off through the labor. At about two to three centimeters, the doctor broke my water. He said the meconium was clear which indicated that whatever had caused our baby's death, happened so fast that if I had headed to the emergency room when it happened, they could not have saved him. This gave me some comfort. He had not suffered for a moment.

At some point, T. arrived. I asked first for Stadol, and when that was not enough, I was given Morphine. Although it was the shortest of my labors by about half, it was the most painful. I cannot describe to someone who has not done it…the difference between birthing a living baby and one who was not. At just about the point I decided I would have an Epidural, the doctor told me I was at nine centimeters. My midwife got me up on my knees and within minutes, I was able to push.

My son was born at 5:19 A.M. on Monday, February 28, 2005.

One of the memories I will be able to cherish is his small, warm body as I pushed it out. He was placed on my belly, wrapped in a warmed towel and I held him and cried. Pictures were taken.

B. had called the pastor at about the time I started pushing and she arrived soon after his birth. She performed a brief naming ceremony and it meant so much to have her lay her hands on him and pray with us at that time. T. had to go. She signed a cross on his head before leaving. She looked at him and said with tears in her eyes, "All he knew was love."

We had time alone with him. About an hour and a half after his birth, it was time to go to the nursery. I refused a wheelchair. We walked, my husband holding one of my hands and the pastor holding the other. He was weighed at four pounds, 13 ounces and measured at 19 inches. So big for 33 weeks! Footprints and handprints were made on a keepsake birth certificate. A little gown and blanket were chosen from the hospital's store.

When I became so tired that I needed to get back to my room, I was given my baby to hold. His hands were so much like A.'s, with the long fingers and he had long feet too! He had M.'s chin and O.'s nose. I couldn't stop kissing his hands and nose. I cried again over him. After I handed him back to the nurse, the pastor walked me back to my room while my husband stayed with baby B. a bit longer.

I slept, and B. went home to shower and spend a few hours with our kids. He offered them the chance to come see their brother, and they chose not to.

After I woke up, the nurse tried to get me to eat. After I refused to pick anything from the menu, she ordered a sandwich and fries and ordered me to eat.

B. came back. We had to fill out the fetal death certificate and contact the funeral home. When it came time for B. to call the funeral home to confirm that they should pick him up, the nurse told him to "tell them you had a fetal demise." He stared at her, picked up the phone and called to confirm the pick-up of "my infant son." I didn't want to...I really didn't want to. Just listening to my husband make arrangements for them to come pick up our baby's body was too hard.

It was almost time to go. The nurse brought us little B. for the last time. I held him and she took pictures of us with him. B. did not feel able to hold him again. Just before I gave him back to the nurse, I kissed his little forehead goodbye. It was so cold.

She had not even wheeled the little crib out of the room before we were sobbing in each other's arms. I got dressed and she brought us the memory box the nursery had prepared for us. The little gown and blanket were there, and a card with a lock of his hair and a locket for it, and a tiny stuffed tiger. We cried again. His big brothers both adore tigers and the oldest one has a huge stuffed one. Having said our goodbyes, we left our baby and returned to the rest of our family.

Three days later, the new pastor left for 10 days to Haiti. We waited until she got back for the memorial as she had met our son and laid her hands on him. She performed a beautiful service and I was quiet touched at one point when she had to stop to compose herself. Most memorials have a "life history." Baby B.'s had a reflection by our midwife on the pregnancy and our family.

Life is surreal. I should still be pregnant. I still feel him kicking. I read that this is normal. We should have had a lifetime with this child. Instead, we have some pictures, a lock of hair and a very small urn in our bedroom. We had considered taking his ashes to California to be buried with his paternal grandma but all of us decided we wanted him with us. We have moments of normality. More of them, but still many moments of tears.

M. summed it up well. "We'll never stop being sad about our baby. He'll always live in a corner of our hearts."

"Catherine"

I am 31 years old. I contracted HPV (Human Papillova Virus) when I was 27. I couldn't believe that I had a sexually transmitted disease. Apparently, you get it from your partner who has HPV or has come in contact with other partners. The doctor said it is hard to have a vaginal delivery so I pretty much gave up on having a child.

When I was 29, I met a marvelous person. He soon became my husband two years later. We decided we would have a family right away. My family was so happy for me since I felt like all hope was gone for a baby of my own.

We got married in September of 2004. We tried to conceive but it just wouldn't happen.

On April 30, 2005, I took a pregnancy test. I knew that it was going to happen. It said, "pregnant." I was so excited. I told my husband while he was watching cartoons. We were so thrilled. He said, 'don't tell anyone until the 12 weeks are up.' I wanted to tell everyone and their dog!

I immediately started having brown discharge. I figured that it was perfectly normal. On May 3, I got another urine test that said it was positive. I was so excited. My husband is a doctor so he knew it was normal and he had started reading books about pregnancy. I ordered two books: "Little Earthquakes" and "The Miraculous World of the Unborn Baby. I also ordered Preggie Pops for morning sickness.

The morning sickness came and left. I felt really good around May 8. I told myself that I didn't feel pregnant at all. I started having more discharge but I ignored it. It wasn't bright red.

I took pre-natal vitamins but they made me so queasy. I heard about Flintstone vitamins and I started taking those. I loved Chinese food so I ate it whenever I got the chance. We flew out to Houston on May 13 for a wedding. We were so happy. We didn't want to tell anyone about the pregnancy. I threw up that weekend and I was so happy to be uncomfortable and sick.

We watched a video on fetus development. We were so excited that week about the big Star Wars 3 movie. I felt fine that week.

On May 20, the panic swept through me. I had already made an appointment for May 25 so I knew that I would see the doctor soon. The blood started that night on May 20. It was bright red. My husband said we should go to the emergency room. I wanted to wait until the next morning. It was spotting but not real bad.

On May 21, we went to get our paperwork done for our house that we are building. The cramps started so my husband took me to Urgent Care. They said that I should go to the hospital.

I got to the hospital and the bleeding was starting to ease up. They said we have to look at the cervix, which was closed. That is always good news, but I was in danger. No one said what kind of danger.

We looked at the ultrasound but my bladder was empty. They did a vaginal ultrasound and the baby looked dead. I didn't believe them. It's not dead. It's just very little. It is .6 mm.

There was nothing they could do. The heartbeat was not there. I was having major cramps and the ultrasound showed the cramping. But no blood was going to the fetus. They did a quantitative HCG. It was 3228. I was only five to six weeks pregnant…very early, compared to the eight weeks I calculated. I knew the baby was dead.

I didn't feel sick or hungry. My breasts were not tender anymore. I had 21 days to feel pregnant.

That night, on May 21, the cramping and bleeding exploded. I was so devastated. Everything was pouring out of me. They gave me an RH shot but they told me there was nothing they could do.

Why? Why did my first have to die? No one really knows. It could have been the dehydration I had felt. Of course, I did not starve or thirst myself to death.

On May 22, the bleeding continued. On May 23, I got a quantitative HCG test again. It was 728. The baby was gone.

I will see the doctor on May 25. It is okay. I quit my job and I can really try to be okay. I am only 31. I can have another kid. I just want one.

"Sara G."

On January 14, 1999, my world changed forever.

It is painful to write about but I want others to hear my story and know that they are not alone, as that is the one thing that gave and continues to give me solace through my infertility struggle. I had had one first trimester miscarriage, then two wonderful children despite my struggles with an incompetent cervix which necessitated a cervical cerclage and bed rest each time.

I was happily pregnant with my third child. The cerclage had gone well the month before and I was at 18 weeks, just beginning to show and to let people know I was pregnant. I am a psychiatrist. I was in the second year of my residency then, working hard on the wards. I finished up with my last patient and raced to my checkup.

My obstetrician was seeing me every two weeks in order to monitor for cervical dilation and it was not always easy to arrive at his office in time for my appointments. As usual, he started the appointment by asking how I was feeling and checking my cervix, which was thankfully closed tightly. He then listened for the baby's heartbeat and his brow furrowed. I did not hear anything on the monitor as he continued to search, muttering "The baby can't be hiding that far away." An ultrasound confirmed that there was no fetal movement and no heartbeat.

The rest of that week is now a blur to me of numbness, shock and tears. Because of my obstetrician's operating schedule, he had me wait the weekend and then performed what is known as a D & E (dilation and evacuation) of my uterus, essentially scooping out my baby. All I remember from that day is watching a woman at full term labor next to me, and crying and crying after my surgical procedure. Testing was done on me and on the "fetal tissue" (my baby!) and no reason was ever found for his death. My obstetrician informed me that such an event was extremely rare and I had no reason to worry about future pregnancies. My biggest regret from that time is that I allowed the D & E rather than delivering and being able to see and hold my son. I think this would have ultimately helped me tremendously in my grieving.

I felt that the world had changed for me. It was no longer a safe place, as I now knew that bad things could happen to me and to my family which could be irreversible. I had nightmares for months afterwards about dying while my children were alone in the house and didn't know what to do, with no one finding them for days and days. I also struggled with explaining the death of their brother to my two living sons, as I had no explanation for myself. How could I expect them to understand?

My husband and I told almost no one of what had happened to us, as very few people knew I was pregnant. We thus cut ourselves off from any source of comfort or support. Deprived of the normal grieving process, I fell into a deep depression which continued throughout the next two years and ultimately required psychiatric intervention which continues today, despite the successful birth of my third child 13 months after my pregnancy loss. I remember that pregnancy as a haze of misery, depression and worry that my baby would die again. It was not until I held my son in my arms that I was sure he would not die during the pregnancy.

When we decided to have our next child, it took four months to achieve a pregnancy. I then suffered another first trimester loss. After a few more months of trying again and being off most of my medications to do so (much of the medication I need to stay well is not safe to use during pregnancy), I began to become more depressed again. We decided to proceed with infertility treatment in order to achieve a pregnancy before I became too ill. Month after month, I took injections, sonograms and had endless procedures done. We spent much money we could not afford. I ultimately became pregnant again after what felt like ages. Understandably, having lost three pregnancies by now, my husband and I were terrified. We worried every day about the pregnancy and breathed a sigh of relief each night when that day had gone okay. But then there was always the next day to worry about and the next, and the next.

The cerclage went well and all was proceeding normally. As the pregnancy approached 18 weeks, we became more and more frightened that our baby would die again. But things went well and I began early on to feel my baby kicking every so often.

At the 18th week, we took a weekend car trip out of town for a family wedding and as recommended, we stopped often for breaks and for me to exercise my legs, to reduce the risk of blood clots developing in them. The weekend started well but I began to worry on Saturday night when I realized that I hadn't felt any movements for a while. I told my husband and we tried to reassure ourselves that it was so early on that I probably just couldn't feel the baby that particular day. Anyway, we were out of town, and there was nothing I could do about it right then. But, of course, we both worried.

Upon returning to town, I went to see my obstetrician the next day just to reassure myself that things were all right. After all, I knew from last time that a second trimester loss was rare and it was unlikely to happen again to me. I had three wonderful children! Sitting on the chair, waiting to be admitted to the examining room, however, I couldn't stop my tears as I was flooded with memories of the last time I had waited at 18 weeks for an ultrasound. When I was finally on the table, my doctor searched for a few minutes for a heartbeat. I was too frightened to watch his face because somewhere, deep inside myself, I believe I knew the answer even before he straightened up and spoke to me.

"This shouldn't be happening, Sara, but I can't find a heartbeat," he said.

"Let's send you to the big ultrasound room down the hall, where they can do a more extensive examination."

The nurses were kind enough to walk me through the back way, as I couldn't stop crying. I knew they would not find a heartbeat and I did not watch the monitor. I did not see the picture on the ultrasound screen of my motionless son and his still heart. It was October 26, 2004.

Again. I walked to my car in a daze. Again, I called my husband in utter disbelief. Again, we sat on the couch in shock and stared at each other. How could this be happening again, when we had expended so much time, money and emotional effort on this baby?

The first 18 week loss was supposed to have been just a fluke, not a pattern. How could our yearned for baby die – again? The great irony was that the major problem with my pregnancies was that I dilated too early because of my incompetent cervix, and again, my cervix was shut tight. All had looked well – except that the baby had inexplicably died.

My initial instinct was to have another D & E so I could get the baby out and deny this had ever happened. But my obstetrician felt that I was too far along and that a D & E would damage my cervix. (I never understood why I had that procedure the first time around.) With the caring, sensitive help of my psychiatrist, I came to understand that I would ultimately feel better to have seen the baby and so the next day, I was admitted for the induction of labor. It took much of the day for my cervix to dilate enough but at 7:00 that night, I delivered my son. He was so small that the contractions were just beginning to get difficult when he was born. I asked to see him and the nurses put him on a receiving blanket and handed him to me.

Just at that time, my wonderful psychiatrist arrived to give me support (my husband could not be there for religious reasons), and together, we looked at the baby. We commented on the perfection of his tiny hands, on how he had no hair yet, but mostly, we just looked. He was perfectly formed with every external organ in place, but he was dead. We looked and just sat with him until my obstetrician needed to take me back to the operating room to remove the rest of the placenta. The nurses took pictures of my son, and I kissed him and handed him back. The anesthesiologist medicated me, and I awoke next during the night. Despite my grief, I remember this time that I was able to spend with my son as being very peaceful, and time that ultimately helped me to begin healing.

My grieving process has been a very painful time in my life, with my depression becoming better and worse at different times. It has been made more difficult by having to make the necessary decision that we cannot have any more children, as I am not able to function at work or at home when I am ill and the risk of remaining off my medications is too great.

We have thought seriously about adoption. As grateful as we are for our three wonderful sons, our family still seems incomplete. But we are still heavily in debt from my infertility treatment and financing an adoption is currently way beyond our means. It's a shame, given all the children out there who need a loving home where they are wanted. We therefore are grieving even more, for our dreams cut short.

We have no medical explanation this time either for why he died. However, this time, I got to hold and bury my baby. My husband and I named him Matanya Yosef. It has helped us to acknowledge that he was a person, not just "fetal tissue." This time, we told our friends and family what had happened and their outpouring of support and caring has been wonderful. I cannot emphasize enough how helpful talking with them and sharing our story has been.

I have a memory album, given to me by a friend, in which I have pasted the sonogram pictures, the photos, the many cards sent to us and other mementos. Matanya's gravesite is marked and I can go back and visit him if I want to. All of this has been very helpful to me in integrating within me what has happened to us.

I am a religious person and for a long time, I was very angry at G-d. I still have many periods where I am angry and rebellious but I have come to some sort of terms with my experience religiously. I have talked to religious friends, I have had a discussion with my rabbi. I have rebelled and have been less and more religiously observant at different times.

I have written poems and have been engaged in intensive psychotherapy with my psychiatrist. All of this has helped me discover me who my post-loss self is and what my identity is, now that I cannot have any more children. It is a heart-wrenching but necessary process which ultimately brings integration of the experience into the rest of my life experiences.

It continues to be sad for me when I care for my pregnant patients but I am now able to help them without feeling overwhelmed for the whole day. I am again able to hold and cuddle and enjoy my friends' babies. What I still do not do well is interact with pregnant women. This holds a special meaning for me that is more difficult to overcome. I wear two rings on my right hand, one for Matanya and one for the other son who died at 18 weeks. I am beginning to integrate the experience. It will always be part of me, as Matanya and my other three babies in heaven will always be part of me.

In closing, I want to share some thoughts which have been helpful to me now that I have been able to read literature of hope without as much anger. I hope that my story is able to help and comfort someone, so that they feel less alone. It has certainly helped me to write and express my pain and my grief.

"Sometimes, the secret lies in making the most music as you can with what you have left."

- violinist Itzchak Perlman, after playing in concert an entire piece with a broken violin string.

"...forgive me
If you are not living
if you, my beloved, my love
if you
have died,
all the leaves will fall on my breast
it will rain upon my soul night and day
the snow will burn my heart,
I shall walk with cold and fire and death and snow
my feet will want to march toward where you sleep,
but
I shall go on living..."

-Pablo Neruda

For Matanya Yosef
 Who died before he had the chance to live

My womb is hollow and bleeding
My breasts shrunken dry, my arms bruised and empty, my mind numb,
But my full heart strains to breaking with each painful contraction,
So deliver unto me all the little children.

The children who cry in the night,
The children who suckle loneliness,
Those who shake with cold, fever, dread, despair,
Guilt, hunger, longing,
Those living and those not given a chance to draw breath,
And those torn from loving arms too soon.

All who yearn for a mother's fond gaze,
A soft touch, a whispered word, a gladdened heart,
Relief from fear, release from shame, protection from all ills,
I will hold them all close and there will be room for all.

So deliver them until my embrace and together we will cry out.
We will storm the heavens together and from our pain demand
Comfort and consolation

Sgg 11/04

The stillbirth

The dough in the mixing bowl rises, gently nudging the towel covering it
      into a soft smooth mound
Which I cup in both palms, thinking of her rounded white sweater and
      her swollen
      Silhouette.
Her three-year-old and my five-year-old on ice skates, her baby kicking
      in her belly
      And mine decaying in the ground; the grass is always greener in
      the cemetery
      Than in her backyard, I suppose.
I knead the dough, working the edges in and in, and teach my son how to
      cut and pinch
      The edges. His eyes light up mischievously as we establish back-
      to-back that
      My inch advantage has shrunk by half.
I close the oven and drape my apron over a floury chair as my middle
      child calls out
      Sleepily for my husband to check on him soon, and it is my turn
      to bestow a
      Kiss.
Why, then, do I soak my pillow with sorry and anger before I can sleep?
      Aren't
      My blessings enough?
True, I long for the smooth round firmness of baby skin, smelling of
      milk and something else indefinable
For the yielding smallness that shapes itself to my body in sleep
For the irresistible smile spilling milk down my chest as the nipple is
      forgotten for
      Play
For the clear-eyed gaze mirroring worshipful adoration
For a body which bursts with the possibilities of life.
Where do I fill my aching arms?
I take the pastry from the oven before it burns, and set it on a rack to cool

for my sons
Who will gobble it in the morning and clamor for more.
Enough! I'll say. You don't want a tummy ache!
And they will leave for school, replete, while I nibble their leftover
    crumbs,
Remembering their babyhood and trying to eat the slice they cut for me.
This is yours, mommy! Don't let it get stale!
As the tears, unbidden, rise!

Sgg 1/05

Consolation

Raindrops glisten through the sunshine as desolate tears and smiles shake
    the heavens.
Smiles for the soul cleansed and tears for my human suffering,
The complex tangle of pain, anger, suffering, guilt, love, compassion
    adding whirls of colored thread
To the awesome tapestry interweaving G-d and man,
The day Matanya returns home to the care of his Creator: tikkun olam.

The child rages, kicking and screaming,
Pounding fists, feet, head,
Writhing in frustration and sorrow on the ground, refusing comfort,
As He looks on in sorrow and compassion, knowing that this must be so
Although His child cannot comprehend, and He aches for the hurt
The day Matanya returns home to the care of his Creator: sorrow.

With great gulping shudders, His child leans warily on His knee,
Aching for comfort but angry at Him and His world.
Sometimes leaning in and sometimes running away as He looks on
    With love
Wanting to comfort but knowing it is too soon and too inexplicable now
The day Matanya returns home to the care of his Creator: compassion

He sends family, friends, therapists, rabbis, to stand by His child's side
And help contain, comfort, listen, and sympathize.
As time passes, His child understands that the answer to her prayers was
        no,
But that He was listening all the while.
She hates it and rages and cries at times, but is able to feel Him cradling
        her
        Lovingly in His arms while she feels what must be felt,
As Matanya Yosef is also cradled in the care of his Creator: consolation.

        Sgg 3/05

"Jane"

<u>Thoughts of the day you should have been born</u>:

Dear fourth baby,

You were my third miscarriage. In some ways, I was more used to it and having a son in the middle helped. As many times as I could, I told people that I have a son. I have a son. I can do it. But deep down, I doubt that I can. As the GP said, I am a Pandora's box of problems. Someone, who many think, should count their blessings and give up.

I am giving up. I am giving up on myself. Abandoning hope. I see the other babies. Your baby friends. There is only you out of our circle of friends. Only you that didn't make it. You had a beating heart, hands and feet. Yet your heart stopped and you remained suspended in your dark waters. I saw you on the scan. Still and ghostly. I was quite happy to keep you there in your stillness. My body did not want to give you up so they put me to sleep and you were sucked out of me. Yet I have carried you every step of this nine month journey. Everywhere I have been, you have been. I have seen all the swollen bellies and I have lied outright. I have pretended you were never there. Pretended I never wanted you. I have felt so jealous but have had to be so interested, kind and fair.

Sometimes, I am optimistic, either about another baby or just about the future, with just us three and the three angels. Sometimes, I am just living but an insensitive comment hurdles me back to my pain. I don't ever want to forget you but sometimes, I wish you would go away. Everyone else thinks you have. *Did I know my due date? Who will give me another great-grandchild? Katie's scan showed a healthy fetus. It is all worth it in the end!* There is nowhere I have been, where I have been safe from a question. *Are you having anymore?* I have not felt safe and relaxed anywhere because every time I have to weigh up the questioner and chose my lie. Sometimes, I lie outright. Sometimes, they know about you but I say it would have been difficult with a toddler. It was probably for the best. I never cry. Never let them dry my tears because what can they say?! There will be more. There may well not be.

And if there is not, how can I make you count? How can I make just a few weeks of a beating heart worthwhile? How can I make them see you are one of my blessings? I don't hate you for dying. I just don't understand why. I hate them…the doctors, for not looking for a reason. They could say, 'look at your son. He is proof.' But do they know how terrified I was every day of his journey? And how much worse it would be now? To be past the point of viability and to still lose.

I am a brave person but I cannot believe how much I have had to endure, just to have one baby. I could maybe try again if I knew what I was up against but to not know is just too cruel.

It was you, the baby that was due today that I wanted. I saw your heart. I wanted you to beat for me. You are not interchangeable. I am tired of trying to be a mummy when I already am. If I risk any more suffering, I may lose my mind. My mind and my body need to be reclaimed back as my own. I have carried four babies. One is asleep upstairs and going to a playgroup this afternoon. The other three are ghosts.

You, number four, were my last
My body knows but it is unacceptable to my mind

How can I not make another to bandage over what was lost?

Number four, I want to carry your photo with me
I want everyone to see you

You were my last
My last

There is nothing wrong with this

I must choose when to stop

When to reclaim myself as myself

And to well and truly count my blessings
Of which number four, you are one.

Your mummy forever, xx

Conclusion

There are so many other stories to tell. Every man and woman has their own story to tell in their own words. Each story is important in its own right and must be told whether it is written down in a private journal or told to a friend, relative or even a total stranger. There is absolutely no shame in having a miscarriage. No one should have to feel alone in his/her pain.

During our time of loss, the people around us – our friends, our family, our co-workers – mean so well when they offer us words of comfort. With the most sincere intentions, they put their arms around us, wipe away our tears and tell us what they think we want to hear.

"It's for the best"

"It was God's way of sparing you a deformed child"

"At least you weren't further along in the pregnancy"

"At least you have other children"

"I know what you're going through"

Having heard every "good wish" in the book, I know that there are really no words that can be said to ease the pain and suffering of a pregnancy loss. Since my own losses, I have spoken with and "counseled" several friends and family members who have experienced a miscarriage. The best thing anyone – whether they have been touched by a miscarriage or not – can say is "I'm sorry" and "I'm thinking of you."

So to every man and woman who has had a pregnancy loss, read these stories over and over again and know that you are not alone. And may you have comfort in knowing that we are all sorry and that we are all thinking of you.